You, Rewritten

By Jamie Sea

MEDICAL DISCLAIMER

We are not, nor are we holding ourselves out to be a

doctor/physician, nurse, physician's assistant, or any other

medical professional. We are not, nor are we holding

ourselves to be your psychologist, psychiatrist,

psychotherapist, or social worker. This content includes

information and instruction relating to wellness topics, such

as relationships, stress, personal growth, etc. You

acknowledge and agree that the following warnings and

disclaimers shall apply to all of the content.

DEDICATION

To my husband, Nick. The one who always has
seen the light in me.

I love you.

-Pook

FORWARD

It is spring of 2014. Both Jamie and I are in places we aren't meant to be forever. As I walked into the building that housed the jobs we each had at the time, I heard the *clack* of a paint brush drop on the ground. As I turned to lend a helping hand, I saw a petite, bright eyed, tattooed woman behind me; she is the coolest person I have ever seen. Jamie is the type of person you are in awe of the first time you meet. Her aura of warmth and comfort permeate from the welcoming smile she shines on every person she passes. I handed her the brush from the ground, *"Thank you!,"* she sang in a voice that sounded like a chirp from a blue bird. She shuffled off down the hall to begin her day. I had no idea that I had just met someone who would change my life forever.

Our friendship has grown into that of a sisterhood. Jamie has held me as I cried, celebrated my wins as a business owner and comforted me through the painful tests the Universe has thrown my way. She has fed me when I didn't feel my body deserved a meal and showed me tenderness when I couldn't be gentle with myself. She has never, for a single second, judged me through any of it.

Jamie is a thoughtful leader, a loving wife and the best mother two little girls could ever ask for. Her journey has been messy, bright, gut wrenching and beautiful. Her businesses have provided jobs, inspiration, and guidance for hundreds of thousands of women throughout the world. She has manifested her dream life and will now teach you to do the same.

You, The Beautiful Reader, are holding a very special book. In it, holds Jamie's story; one she has re-written, despite what society has told her to be. It is a story that is stitched together with threads of hope, faith and trust. Her family and I have watched her pour her heart into the pages you now hold in your hand.

You will learn from her story, as so many of us have, that the only thing that is certain in life, is that you hold the pen.

Jamie is not just my friend, she is yours now, too. You can pick up this book any time you are feeling scared, broken or unsure. Read through it and be reminded that *any damn thing is possible.*

Jamie will love you though wherever it is you are on your journey.

Love,

Simone McMahon, LE

CONTENTS

INTRODUCTION

If you have ever wanted to break out of the box that society has put you in, you've come to the right place.

If you have ever craved a sense of belonging, then this is your book. If you have ever thought, *"I know I have been created for more."* I'll prove to you that you always were.

Cheers to this journey, let's start it together.

Xoxo, Jamie Sea

Chapter One/
Be the change you wish to see.

"When I dare to be powerful, to use my strength in the service of my vision, then it becomes less and less important whether I am afraid." -Audre Lorde

It all started with a bracelet.

I was 22 years old when I received this bracelet as a birthday present. It had a thin brown leather strap that was connected to a silver circle. On it, was a message stamped in metal.

"Be the change you wish to see in the world."

A year later, I sat in the ICU with my head on my brother's heart as we let him off of life support. The sound of the beeping machines, tears and heavy sobbing from my family echoed through the room while I remained entirely numb. I watched him lie there, my big strong brother, my best friend, who was now with the angels. As each family member walked out of the room, I sat there, reluctant to leave him just yet. I glanced over to my patient fiancé, who remained quiet by the door with his hands clasped. He nodded to me as if to say, *"take as much time as you need."*

I sat there with my brother, and I untied my bracelet from my wrist and tied it to his. With my hand on his, I promised him that I would take care of my family.

This event dramatically changed my life, but most importantly and unbeknownst to me at the time, it would change the way my brain would function. It changed how I would make decisions and all of my actions thereafter. At my brother's service, I watched his children stand there holding their mother's hand, crying because they would never see their father again. I watched my father cry because he would never see his son again. And there I stood, emotionless.

Not one fucking tear.

I still didn't cry the next day or the day after that, or even the day after that. So, what do you do when you feel nothing? You go back to what you know— whatever your normal is. And for me, that was work. I was a hairstylist at the time and I went in full force, working all the damn time so I could prevent any emotions from surfacing. To stay numb, it was necessary for me to also rely heavily on drinking what ended up being too much wine at night. Grief, plus work, plus excessive drinking was the way I handled it. Months and months passed and I felt nothing, so I thought, "*YES! I successfully avoided the feelings of trauma and grief.*"

But boy, was I wrong. So freakin' wrong.

Let's talk scientifically about what happened to me during that time: My subconscious mind (which I will tell you more about very soon) went straight to work when Scotty died and immediately began to protect me. It suppressed the horrifying things I witnessed and tucked them away within the depths of my mind.

The result? Numbness.

The funny, not so funny thing is: that's where my healing lived, that's where my success lived, and that's most certainly where my fear lived. All of this was stored in my subconscious mind and I avoided it for way too long.

Looking back to where I grew up in Bristol, Connecticut, houses in my neighborhood were similar to a raised ranch and built close to one another. The streets were quite busy, and I remember having so much fun playing outside in the backyard with my Dad tossing a softball while the cars whizzed by. In elementary school, I remember having a birthday party where my parents hired a guy to be Barney, the purple dinosaur, and I recall feeling absolutely mortified.

All the children were thrilled at getting the chance to meet and hug Barney, all while I was horribly embarrassed thinking, "*I'm not a damn baby anymore!*"

I realize now how extraordinary my parents were and how they went out of their way to make me feel so special. Every year, we would have these big beautiful birthday parties where we would have music, food, games and, of course, the man-made slip n' slides. We would anchor down huge tarps, dump a bottle of shampoo and my Dad would man the hose while we catapulted down the slide like wet seals. During summer, my Dad was known for always hosting these amazing family parties with the volleyball net set up, The Steve Miller Band blasting through the radio and, of course, a ton of jello shots.

I can see now that my parents played a huge role in shaping my beliefs. My mom was in the clothing industry and worked as a retail manager. My dad, on the other hand, worked in the machinery industry and worked really freakin' long hours. I learned my work ethic from both of them as they always put in extra effort, showed up on time, really cared for their job, and set goals they wanted to achieve. Even though my dad worked much longer hours than my mom, no matter what, he always came home at night through that heavy sliding door with a smile and was ready to love us to pieces.

I vividly remember my mom wanting my sister and I to have the best shoes and outfits so that we would feel like we fit in. My mom is seriously amazing and truly wanted the best for us, and is still the same to this day. Even with all of that effort, I started feeling completely lost by the time I hit 15. I fell in love with the idea of becoming a drummer, maybe because my big brother was a kickass drummer, maybe because the boy I had a crush on in middle school was a drummer in the school band, or maybe because my family played in a band in my basement when I was a kid.

Nevertheless, I had a huge draw to be in the school band and learn how to play music. I gathered up the courage to ask my Mom and was shut down at lightning speed.

"Nerds play drums in the school band. And you aren't a nerd."

At that moment, a new belief was in infancy, ready to bury its way into my subconscious mind. I contorted this construct that to be accepted, I had to be someone that my parents wanted me to be. More and more events would occur that would push me further from being the authentic artist I craved to be. I became someone I didn't even recognize and the continuous masking of my spirit would turn destructive. I developed a secret eating disorder by the age of 16, which sadly destroyed my self-worth, self-image, and ability to think clearly. To cope with years of suppressed emotions, I was rebelling and being resistant, which resulted in depression, a smaller unhealthy body, and daily panic attacks.

My parents also believed that the best way to accomplish a successful career was to go to college, score high grades, and land a kick-ass, high-paying job. Maybe they believed this because they never went to college and they simply wanted their kids to have more opportunities than they did.

My poor parents...I gave them a run for their money. I hated school, got pretty awful grades, spent most of my high school career like a drunken idiot. And then, on top of that, I told them I wanted to become a hairstylist. My parents' perception of me becoming a hairstylist was, *"That's not what smart women do."* (Spoiler alert: I ended up landing a kick-ass, high-paying job as a hairstylist.)

I was always really drawn to being a creative person, so the idea of college made me sick to my stomach. The concept of sitting in a classroom all day was soul-sucking, when, in reality, all I really wanted to do was paint, create or learn to play music.

At times, I didn't want to get out of bed because of my eating disorder and depression. I'd have a thought about how my pants fit, end up crying in the mirror for hours and not want anyone to see me for weeks on end. Looking back, I feel so sad for that version of myself. She had no concept of why she felt the way she did, she just felt sad, lost, and unlovable.

That's the thing about the formation of beliefs: they start small, build a home in your mind and, over time, it becomes who you believe you are. I now had developed a firm belief and understanding of who I authentically craved to be: the artist, the musician, the girl with piercings and tattoos, was in fact, unlovable. I grew up believing this until I learned how mindsets work, and how to tap into my highest self, and BAM! Everything changed. I now stand proudly as that artist with the tattoos and piercings, lovable as fuck.

A growth mindset is about rewiring your past experiences and relearning your understanding of a situation or incident. To this day, I have taken many events of my life and their outcomes and picked out the positive aspects, what I learned, and its impression on my life. I've learned to rebuild my self-worth, self-compassion, optimism and hell, even healed my eating disorder.

As I started to learn more about the spirit and mindsets, I could feel the difference in my life. I realized that talent and intelligence are traits that can be accentuated with intention and commitment, which means you can take a perceived problem and instead view it as a challenge— something that is achievable vs. impossible. Living up to expectations is a fear that has been instilled in most children, which, in return, reflects their deciding power and how they live the rest of their life. With the right effort, a person can conquer the world and soak in information by approaching a problem with enthusiasm to fight the difficulties instead of being fearful of them.

What is a smart woman, really? I believe a smart woman is someone who listens to her spirit, follows her passion and unlearns all the shit she believes to be true about her potential. She may fall, but she stays determined and comes back up with a lesson she has learned from the experience. By accentuating her strengths, she shows the world she has more to offer than what might be expected of her. By remaining in alignment versus hustle, a woman can be anything that she damn well pleases. All while finding blissful balance. There isn't anything a woman can't do when she encourages herself, heals her pain, and then remembers she was always made whole.

Here's a fun fact: when you are young, your mindset is being formed as you grow. From the ages of zero to seven, you are a sponge, taking in everything you are told as truth.

You have no conscious awareness to say to someone, *"Hey, wait one freakin' second, that story sounds made up."* You just accept it all as truth, believe it and store it all as data in your robot brain. You are taught the concept of love, happiness, money, success, and worthiness through your life experiences that now creates the person you show up as today.

To access the highest and most magnetic version of yourself, I will teach you how to reframe your perceived "failures" by imagining your letdown in a positive light. Think of one now, and write down, *"What did this teach me? What did I learn from this setback? How did it allow me to think differently?* Highlight your setbacks and understand them with a refined approach. When you can view it as an opportunity to re-approach, you will find it easier to then drench yourself in some delicious self-compassion. (An essential ingredient to your self-growth.)

I remember writing a letter to myself at the age of 14; I was confident, joyful, and was absolutely sure of how my life would turn out. Then, by age 16, I was a vastly different human. I wasn't the confident person anymore who could own the room as soon as they walked into it. I didn't know how to take action even when it was crucial for me to do so. I felt I no longer radiated the energy that would hold attention for too long or had an aura that was emitted by a charismatic personality, even though my Mom would say otherwise. By the time I left cosmetology school at age 19, I knew I had the potential to achieve more but always felt limited by the idea of making more income. Honestly, I had a crap relationship with receiving money, very little self worth, and after years of allowing myself to not receive what I deserved, I came to the concrete conclusion that I would be this way forever.

See, that's the thing. When you aren't aware of mindset, manifestation, or soul work, you feel stuck in your perceived final form, with no way to escape. I always thought that my life was just going to be bare minimum until I actually made a new choice. And that choice was to admit that being broke sucks. Like really really really sucks. And I didn't want to live that way anymore. Actually, the real reason I decided I didn't want to be broke anymore was that I became a mother. The moment I met the absolutely amazing human I created, I thought, *"Fuck that, I need to provide more for her. She deserves that; my family deserves that."* At this point, I decided to buck up, put my big girl pants on and learn how to change my beliefs, paradigms, identity and concentrate on how to take action. I learned to expand my mind, body, and soul. I managed to do it all with four bucks to my name, a newborn baby, a hot husband, and a good dose of debilitating postpartum depression. Little did I know, a millionaire was in the making (a really happy and fulfilled one might I add).

Six months after my brother Scotty departed, I married my best friend, Nicholas. I was working full time as a hairstylist and Nick was working for his father as an electrician. Hair had been something I had loved ever since I was 13 years old, so to be doing it as a full-time job was pretty incredible. For 8 years, I stayed at the same salon, barely making ends meet, working long hours but still not being able to afford much.

I eventually went on to sell my belongings to pay for groceries, I sold my car and downgraded my cell phone all while my husband worked a second job as a janitor at our local Catholic school. We declined family vacations, refused to look at our barely-there-bank account, and the one thing we were always able to attend were our evening panic attacks.

It wasn't until 2013, when our beautiful Charlotte Scott was born, that everything changed. The moment I laid eyes on her, something in my heart shifted, and I knew, as her momma, I needed to make a better life for her. I didn't care what it took, and I refused to struggle, to cry about bills, and to not offer her the life experiences she deserved. At that moment, success was the only option.

5 months later, I mustered up the courage to leave my safe salon job and go into business for myself. I had put in my two weeks and was banking on my last paycheck to cover the costs of my first month's rent at the new salon I was going to be working at. My former salon owner called me on my day off and told me never to come back and that all my belongings would be mailed to me. 8 years of relationships gone in an instant and without warning. And that last paycheck? That was gone too.

My heart sank. It was that initial feeling of, "*OMG! WHAT THE FUCK DID I JUST DO TO MY FAMILY?*"

I had nothing to my name, not one penny. So as I was hyperventilating and wiping the snot from my face, I gathered the courage to call my father.

"*Dad, I have nothing.*"

I actually assumed he would yell at me or tell me I shouldn't have left my job and should have known that this is what happens when you put your family at risk. But what he actually said next was the best thing I have ever heard.

"*J-birdy, you are healthy and that's all that matters. I'll give you just enough to pay rent, then you pay me back as soon as you get back on your feet.*"

I felt humiliated to take the money from him, but in the same breath, I was so relieved and even more motivated to make shit happen so I could pay back every single penny ASAP.

As for my husband? He should win a damn award. He has always believed in me and trusted my choices, which I thought was admirable, since he was struggling just as much with anxiety, working two jobs, and helping raise a baby. Little did I know, the success that was on the horizon would allow him to come up for air in ways we would have never imagined.

My Dad gave me enough to pay my first month's rent and I was left with 4 dollars in my name. FOUR DOLLARS. But most importantly, I was left with the mindset that failure was not an option, and it was at that exact moment that I unknowingly activated the many laws of the universe.

Let's fast forward 7 years later: I opened two successful million dollar companies, a very lucrative coaching business, and it didn't take me long to understand how it all happened. I wasn't just *"one of the lucky ones,"* I profoundly believed in the inevitability of my success, helping people, chasing joy, and taking messy, yet inspired action.

The subconscious mind is powerful and mysterious as it holds the vastness of our minds' inner workings. If you know what is going on in your brain, it gets much easier to be more mindful of what could be standing in the way of a life you didn't even know was possible for you. The subconscious mind or, as I call it, *"the robot brain,"* is the head honcho of your life. It shows up every day to run the show to ensure you think the same, act the same, and make things scary as hell if you want to do something new in your life or your business. Before I make the robot brain out to sound like the bad guy here, I'd like to share with you its real main goal. The head honcho only wants to keep you alive. Here is the amazing news: you can actually change and rewire your robot brain. It's called neuroplasticity, and it's the ability of the brain to adapt to changes in an individual's environment by forming new neural connections over time. So simply put, you have the opportunity right now to have your mind become your built-in bestie and hype girl instead of the nagging negative enemy that rents a very expensive room in your head.

To fully achieve and harness the potential of making this part of your mind the best friend you want for life, you want to do something that sounds fairly simple. Become wildly aware. You will choose to look within and make a decision that a limited mindset or fixed mindset is no longer serving a purpose and that you have the power to change the way you think, and in turn, change the way you show up in the world. You are not stuck. I repeat, you are not stuck. You may feel that way right now, but stick around with me, and I'll show you how it's possible. (Pinky promise, it's worth it.)

So, at this point, you must be thinking, "*How?*"

Here is the truth: changing the way your mind functions takes intention and softness. You must start by giving yourself permission to dig deeper within and study each of the significant events that have happened in your life, observe your way of being, and how you process and react to certain situations. Your hidden beliefs, which depict and give direction to your future actions, need to be identified. Fears often become true as your unconscious mind usually starts propelling the negative self-talk into real-life outcomes; thus, awareness is your first step. Become wildly aware. That's my challenge to you in this book. Put away your fear, your self-doubt, your ideas of what you can and can't do or be, to pause to observe and become aware of your story. I've shared my story with you, and now it's time to take a look at yours.

Let's do the damn thing.

Chapter Two/
The Story of You and Your Subconscious Mind

"You may not control all the events that happen to you, but you can decide not to be reduced by them." -Maya Angelou

I was 15 when I got my hair done by a professional hairstylist for the first time. I had begged my Mom to let me get bright blonde highlights and after a ridiculous amount of convincing, she begrudgingly agreed and let me get a DIY highlighting kit from the supermarket. My older sister was responsible for applying the color and I vividly remember sitting legs crossed in the kitchen with a beaming smile as my sister, with absolutely zero prior knowledge of applying highlights, began to do her best. An hour later, my utter excitement would soon turn to defeat and a puddle of tears. What I had anticipated to be a beautiful honey hue would actually result in uneven stripy, brassy blorange highlights.

The next step? My first trip to see a professional hairstylist. As I walked into the hair salon for the first time, I remember being in awe as I looked at the hairstylists thriving in their creativity and working their magic. I couldn't believe that it was an actual job, and hairstylists could make a living by creating art and talking to people to form deep, meaningful connections. And what happened, then? Well, you know in Whoville how they say, "the Grinch's small heart grew three sizes that day." Well that's what happened to mine that day, too. I knew, without a doubt in my being, I was meant to be a hairstylist.

At 15, I surely wasn't aware of the stigma of the beauty industry. There was, however, a stereotype that my parents believed, and it was this: being a hairstylist and being wealthy didn't go hand-in-hand. Of course, they wanted me to be successful and what do most people think you need to do to achieve that? Get good grades in high school so that you can get a scholarship to go to college so that you can land a solid, steady career that you will work in for the next 20-30 years of your life. Low risk, work for someone else in a steady 9-5. But what they didn't understand yet was that I craved more.

As I continued to grow and mature, my belief system was continually being shaped and molded by external factors. On an unconscious level, I started to form a deep belief that I had to embody the identity of the person my parents wanted me to be. I believed I had to be successful, that I had to work hard to receive an abundance of money, and there were very few paths that I could actually choose for my life that would lead me to success. I don't think these beliefs are unusual or unheard of. Actually, I believe they are quite common and they are developed over time by whoever is raising us with their own limitations and beliefs, mixed with societal expectations, and personal experiences.

I know you have similar beliefs within your subconscious mind that are also at work in your life. You may or may not be aware of these beliefs yet, but during this book, I will be providing you with tools to access them and rewire them.

By the time we reached alpha brainwave function at 12 years of age, your subconscious had confirmed belief systems within your mind that would go on to shape your emotions and actions until this day. What is this subconscious mind that I'm talking about? I'm sure you've heard of your subconscious mind. It's not a groundbreaking truth to tell you that you have one and that it has an effect on you. But what may be more surprising is just how much your subconscious mind controls the outcome and success of your goals and plans.

It is important to think of your subconscious mind as a separate person from you. And that you are your subconscious mind's only priority. Its job is to ensure that you respond exactly the way you are programmed. Your subconscious mind makes everything you say and do fit a pattern consistent with your self-concept.

The unfortunate thing is that your subconscious mind can't tell the difference between the truth and a lie. It can't think independently, everything that it knows is based on the things that you have experienced throughout your life, and specifically from years 0-12.

Your submind doesn't know the difference between personal experience and what is actually true. Maybe you saw the people who raised you struggle with money and you know that they didn't go to college, so you believe that college is the answer to financial difficulties. Maybe you watched your best friend get pregnant and have a baby at a young age. You may have seen her struggle emotionally and witnessed how her whole life shifted from pursuing what she originally had wanted, and now, as an adult, you believe that having children will weigh you down and prevent you from accomplishing your goals and the life you've built for yourself.

When your submind is misinformed and is believing lies, it's as if you have an overprotective parent in your head who can't tell what's true and what's false and who is holding you back from everything that you need and want because it believes it's bad.

Your submind, which consists of 95% of your brain power, is running as fast as it can toward the things that it believes are true and good. This doesn't just apply to your beliefs around your business or future business, this applies to literally everything. Including money, wealth, self worth, love, abundance, and success. Whatever your submind believes, that is what is fueling your action taking and results in every area of your life.

So, even though you don't realize it, every aspect of your life is now guided by your beliefs that you've learned throughout your life. Whether it's self-love or your career choice, your subconscious mind is like the supercomputer of your life, and it is keeping you from the things that it believes are bad for you. Your life is held captive by whatever it is that your subconscious mind believes to be true.

Here is where self-sabotage comes in. You may have experienced this in the form of procrastination, perfectionism, excuses, or assuming a negative outcome attached to the thing you actually want. It's very common for people to self-sabotage their goals and this happens as a result of the beliefs that are within your submind. Here is how it works: take, for example, your perspective on love. Let's say you watched the people that raised you go through a tumultuous divorce when you were young. All of the things around that experience were stored within your submind, and your beliefs on love were beginning to be shaped.

As you witnessed the pain and hurt surrounding this experience, your robot brain was busy watching. It stored up all of these memories and the ways that it made you feel and began to shape your beliefs around love. Remember, as I stated before, from the ages of 0-12, your mind is a sponge and takes everything in as TRUTH. You are continuously learning so you won't get hurt, and your robot brain is in charge of it all. You learn to tie your shoes to avoid the pain of tripping and scraping your knees. Similarly, you also store beliefs about love that remain within your mind until you become an adult.

"Love is temporary, it doesn't last."

"Tie my shoes or I'll trip"

"True love doesn't exist."

"Love will hurt me."

"Love is painful. Love is bad."

Truths were mixed in with lies, and your brain, as a child, didn't know the difference. These experiences turned into beliefs, which then turned into thoughts and actions. Your mind believes that love is bad and will hurt you, and now it is working to avoid love. This manifests as fear of commitment, being afraid to be loved, and being scared to be vulnerable, etc. This can occur even if it's an unconscious belief.

Your robot brain is running 95% of your life. It's meant to serve and protect you, but it's influenced by all the things that you experienced as a child and learned throughout your life. So now, you have this entire belief system that makes up your perspective on yourself, the world and, most importantly, love.

So, remember those beliefs we just talked about?

"Love is temporary, it doesn't last."

Because of your childhood experiences, your subconscious mind now believes that if I fall in love, it won't last, and I will get hurt in the end. So fast forward to being an adult, you're in a relationship and things are going really well. Your 5% conscious mind is like, *"OMG, I think I might love this person!"* And then your overly protective robot brain starts whispering, *"OMG, NO! NO LOVE. Girl, you told me love was bad. You're going to get hurt. Don't you remember?? ABORT! ABORT! ABORT!"* And suddenly, you find yourself picking fights, becoming jealous for no reason, and you end up breaking up. Then again, proving the belief system to be correct that love is bad and won't last. Ingraining that belief system even deeper into your neural network and spiritual energetic system.

You're not sure why you always push people away. You don't understand why you never seem to stay in a good relationship. The answer is that you pushed love away because underneath the surface, deep within your subconscious, you believed that love was bad for you.

In order to grow, there is a need to unlearn the false limits you believe. You must know, these limits feel real...really freaking real. But I promise you, whatever thoughts or ideas you believe to be true, will be. Understand that there are so many things you have been told through personal experiences, societal expectations, and people in your life that have crafted a mind that is now all yours. If you could choose to think about yourself and your ability differently, would you? Because whether you see it or not, you are not broken and nothing needs fixing. You are a light that is unique, born beyond perfect, and is supposed to shine. I am rooting for you to be the person you were born to be because being held back by limiting beliefs and fear only confines you and restricts your potential to make your life something beautifully spectacular.

Unveiling your true authentic self is a wild ride but absolutely beyond worth it. To truly discover your authenticity, you should understand your robot brain and how it takes in information and inherently creates stories around your beliefs, ideas of abilities, who you are, and what you think you can achieve. If you decide to bravely take the route to rewrite your old stories and reframe them to create new neural networks inside the brain, you will find that you can eventually show up as your most divine self and start to create more purpose-driven success, fulfillment, and joy for yourself. In contrast to feeling that you have to be someone else's version of success, you can trust your decision-making and inner knowledge. Instead of feeling stuck and unsure of how to move forward or grow, you take the initiative with intuitive trust. Later on in this book, I'll share with you the science of building self-confidence. But for now, I want to share what has been most helpful, not only for myself, but for my community of female entrepreneurs that I coach.

First, the strongest habit one can pick up is communicating at the right time, with themselves and then with others. I will teach you how to become the observer of your inner narrative, which will allow you to take soulful action instead of remaining fearful of the what-ifs from the ego space. Secondly, it's crucial to discover your strengths (I'm sure you have a TON!), recognize the areas you want to improve, enlighten yourself with your traits in crisis mode, and protect your energy. Lastly, believe that there is a solution to each of the difficulties you may be facing, reframe the thoughts that are holding you back, and believe that your success is inevitable.

The mindset of the people that I grew up with was to stay in the constructed limits that they had developed within themselves, which were adapted due to external factors. Their beliefs were firm on what they knew they could achieve; politics, their favorite baseball team and so on. Now that I firmly understand how the mind cultivates its belief systems, I get how the people I was raised by believed what they did. From what I've gathered, it can be broken down into four categories; who they were raised by, traumatic experiences, repetitive consumption of society and media, and the people they surround themselves with the most.

As an empath, I feel for anyone who thinks they are stuck— who feels they are in their final form and that's simply it. Since I've experienced these exact feelings and thoughts to now being on the other side, I gotta say, you're really going to want to stick around for the rest of this book.

Not just because I kinda know my shit, but also because I want you to experience the feeling of knowing you are limitless.

My mindset being limited and constricted played a huge role as I was growing up, yet when I decided to unlearn my false limitations and get in touch with my highest self, I began to see the world with a new expansive perspective. I began to see changes in my life when I refused to let hardships dictate it. Growing up as a woman, it is easy to fall into the trap of brainwashing by society, the media, and friends/family to be a certain way and to look a certain way. I mean, if only there had been a voice of reason when I was younger that could have assured me that I was allowed to be uniquely myself. That I was worthy, and divinely perfect...

So, for you, my friend, we need to figure out what your story is. I don't want to know your mom's story or your dad's story. I don't care about what your BFF thinks is true or what your grandma thinks you should be doing. I want to know YOUR story. What beliefs are YOU carrying? What important figures in your life helped to shape your belief system? Are any of those beliefs sabotaging your success?

After we can identify the answers to these questions, then we can begin to unlearn the illusions, and release the expectations of others that you've been trying to measure up to. It's going to take work. It might be fucking painful. You may have to bring past trauma back to your mind for the sake of working through it and healing from it. It might get messy, but when it's all said and done, you will have more inner strength, more peace, and more freedom to move fully into the life that is waiting for you.

In the end, I decided not to pursue the traditional style of going to college, getting a degree, and working a normal 9-5 job. And I soon realized that it was the best decision of my life. I no longer felt trapped or felt the need to fit in into a construct that was created by society. Even though people in my life made numerous efforts to get me to go to college, I knew cosmetology school was exactly where I belonged. It was just me. Hairstyling fueled my passion, which made me grow as a person and made my life a lot more joyful.

I'm not here to say that it was all easy peasy once I decided the path I wanted to take. I busted my ass, learned to fight against self sabotage, released the limitations that others placed on my life, and eventually learned to make my subconscious mind my best friend instead of the enemy.

I'll be honest, there will be moments when you doubt your abilities and viciously revisit all your past fuck-ups but it's your next step after those thoughts that truly matter. When you take that first step to become wildly aware, you are at the brink of growth. Do I believe you will achieve your goals? Hell yes. Do I believe that you will have negative thoughts? For sure. Will you then learn to reframe it and then clap for your damn self when you rise up from that? Yes, and yes. See, all that is required for you to be where you want to be is this: make the choice, and open yourself up to the magic of your unlimited potential.

When I first began to slowly and steadily see results, I felt a rush of different emotions taking over me. It was relief, joy and then contentment, all in that order. I knew I wouldn't have to go back to having only four dollars in my pocket. Trusting my inner knowledge and silencing my scary inner narrative is what led me to believe that success was inevitable. And that is exactly where I want to guide you: to the place where you are fully unblocked, and living in your highest power. Even though situations may be tough and you may feel demotivated, stuck, or lost, remember that there is bravery in taking just one step. Take that one small step. Just take it and you will feel a whole lot different, I promise. Take it one day at a time, and learn to be still in your journey. Every step you take, whether forward, backward, big or small, is a part of this path and part of your success story. It's not how fast you can reach the end destination, but the beauty of the path which it took to get there.

I often think about my brother Scott and wish he was here physically. I miss him every day, and hope he sees me holding onto my promise of being the change. I promise to be the change for you, my friend. The soul that will guide you to discover your light, to find joy, and build a purpose-driven business and life, no matter what limiting thoughts may be holding you back.

Chapter Three/
The Universe Within

"In the midst of the winter, I find within me the invisible summer."
-Leo Tolstoy

Alright, we've got your subconscious mind down. Now let's go a little deeper to explore two distinctive parts of you. One of these parts is the story keeper of all that you have been told to believe, the things that you have experienced, and the characteristics that you now identify as. This is called your ego. Not to be confused with "egotistical", as they are definitely not the same.

This "ego" or "false self" is actually made up of many different beliefs you have acquired throughout your life. The other part of you found within your whole being is what I call the "True Self," universe, or God within. This is your spirit and I can take a hard bet that you have some life experience with both your ego and spirit, whether you have realized it yet or not. Both the ego and the spirit are within you, and for most people, they listen to their ego.

Here's an example for you. Let's say you just got off the phone with your best friend and you cannot believe she had the audacity to say that to you. Who does she think she is? Why does she think she can talk to you like that?! EXCUUUUSE ME!? She sure knows how to push your buttons, and you just know she's doing it on purpose.

Even though you may not realize it, your spirit and ego are already at war with each other. The narration that you hear going on in your mind right after that call is from your ego. Your ego is concerned with protecting you. She was so wrong and now you feel the need to argue. Maybe make her feel the same pain you felt, let her HAVE IT. Wouldn't that be fair and just? Wouldn't that make you feel appeased?

After you think about it and cool off after a while, you begin to remember the things she has been going through lately. A different narrative begins to enter your mind. Maybe if you were in her shoes, you would have done the same thing. Felt the same emotions, and maybe even said the same things. Maybe she didn't really mean it, and you should call her back. Be the bigger person and let it go. After all, isn't that what would be best for your friendship and for your friend?

I mean, of all people, you know exactly what she's going through. You know that instead of judging her or being triggered by her words, you can choose compassion, understanding and restoration. You can choose to open yourself up and love her when she needs it the most.

This narrative is from your spirit and it's rooted in love. As these two narratives are going on in your mind, you may not even realize the root or source of each of these thoughts. But even if you don't realize it, you will always choose to listen to only one of them.

Before I began my healing journey, I didn't even realize I had these subconscious thoughts. I had no concept of any of it or how deeply complex it all was. I just heard the disempowering thoughts and limits, and ran with it. I didn't know I had a choice. Because I wasn't aware, I was constantly triggered, living with my eating disorder, and broke as shit. I thought that life was happening to me! The moment I knew I had a choice, I chose differently because living with joy felt possible for once. When you know better, you do better.

Your ego and spirit are two completely different systems of thought that are fighting for space to exist. Your ego is a lower order of reality that is synonymous with fear, sickness, confusion, separation, suspicion, protection, and exclusivity. Your ego wants to protect you in some weird kinda way and it's actually really beautiful if you think of it in that light. It also becomes very helpful to think this way when you need to forgive yourself for the past. A part of me was simply protecting another part of me, and it did the best it could. And now, that part of me no longer serves a purpose here. I can give her love and set her free.

Now let's go back to the best friend example: the fear-based part of your brain remembers the last time that this friend talked to you this way, and it remembers the pain that it caused you. So, out of self preservation, your ego believes that the best thing for you to do would be to cut her out of your life, ignore her, or argue. Whatever it takes to protect you!

Your spirit, on the other hand, is a higher order of reality that is full of love, wholeness, expansion, growth, light, reason and understanding, compassion, and forgiveness. Your spirit can see the big picture. It isn't jaded by the past, but makes decisions from a space of wholeness and love. Your spirit will remind you of what is true. Not just your truth, but the truth that can be found inside of yourself when you are still and listening. Your spirit is what is going to keep you centered and grounded when life gets wild. It keeps you at peace—loving and accepting those around you.

Your spirit is full consciousness and you can hear it when you slow down and move past the energizer bunny speed of your ego, which is the part of you that gets riled up as soon as you're thrown for a loop. When you are still, calm and put yourself in a place to listen, that is when you will be able to hear the voice of the "true self," spirit, universe, or God within you.

The biggest issue is that, most of the time, we are not even aware of this war going on within our subconscious mind and being. Our subconscious is responsible for around 95 percent of our thoughts, so that means that you are only aware of the other 5 percent. The ego and spirit can be fighting for our attention and a decision for one over the other is made before we even realize which we have let win. If we were aware of the voice of our ego and able to identify it when thoughts pass through our minds, then we would be more equipped to kick those thoughts out and listen to the voice of reason that is coming from the spirit.

Hearing the voice of the ego usually comes most naturally and what we listen to most often, because it is usually the loudest. But the voice of the spirit is what we have to learn from within. Once we realize that we have a choice between the two, that is when we can recognize that we need support! And our support comes from the spirit. When we recognize these feelings, we are able to clearly see that we need that guidance. When we go to that secret, quiet place and learn to be still and listen, that is where the spirit can change our minds and perspectives from brokenness to wholeness, from dark to light, from bitterness to love. This is what we call mindfulness. Being aware of what is going on in our minds so that we can take our thoughts captive and choose to listen only to the ones that serve us.

Doesn't this sound so simple?! It is simple, and it takes intention and consistency to instill these habits into your life. You may think this sounds impossible, especially if that inner narrative is too loud or if your personality is naturally of a higher energy. Stillness and mindfulness is something that EVERY personality has the ability to learn and it is one of the most fulfilling and beneficial things that you can do for yourself. It allows you to make decisions with your full mind, and benefits not only your own peace of mind (couldn't we all use more of that?) but it also benefits your relationships, your friends and family, and your community, because you are able to love with your whole being.

So what exactly is mindfulness? It is simply becoming aware of what we are thinking. Pausing, and becoming wildly aware. The space, stillness, taking a breath, relaxing our shoulders, slowly becoming in tune with what it is that your spirit is speaking to you. Practicing mindfulness could look like folding laundry and thinking only about the laundry. Folding it well. Practicing gratefulness that you have clean clothes for work, or for the chubby feet that need all the tiny baby socks. Even just simply focusing on the texture or fabric and how it feels in your hands. Mindfulness is not rushing frazzled through each load with a grumble under your breath. It's a still, peaceful heart that is invested in the present moment. You can practice with yoga, go on a walk, or chat with one of your best friends. You can even practice on the job, doing housework, or cooking a meal. Whatever it is that you are already doing, practice with that.

This is something that I also teach my students in my 1:1 coaching and self-study programs; allowing the thoughts to come in. Do not judge them, or rush them away. Become aware of them. Like I said before, WILDY AWARE. Awareness of these thoughts is the biggest step and is a learned behavior. When the thought enters, acknowledge its presence and look at it objectively. Where is this thought coming from? Is it helpful? Is it an old thought based on something I'm experiencing? How does that thought think it's protecting me?

This will take your commitment and your willingness to put in time and effort to learn this skill! But it's totally worth it. Honestly, this is how I changed my life and the lives of thousands of other female entrepreneurs. You may even think that you don't have the time that it takes to practice mindfulness, but the truth is that you don't have time NOT to.

This is all a process and starting later won't be any more simple than just starting now. You may not see results on the first day, but there will be results. There aren't always physical results, but there are always inward shifts that you will notice as you begin to decipher and differentiate between your ego and the spirit when you find yourself in trying situations. You can't serve two masters. You can't serve ego and spirit. They will both be fighting for space in our minds, but it is ultimately our decision to choose which one we listen to.

Let's talk for a minute about your subconscious mind a little more in depth, shall we? You know you have a subconscious mind by now, but you probably haven't given it much thought before this and you might not realize just how much of your life is run by your subconscious mind. The job of your subconscious mind is this: to store and retrieve data, and to ensure that you respond exactly the way that you should. Your subconscious mind doesn't think or reason independently, it simply obeys the commands that it receives from your conscious mind. It's basically a computer that does what it is programmed to do.

As I've stated before, your subconscious mind also creates 95% of your reality. Your brain works on thought patterns which have been embedded into your neural network. Your beliefs then birth your thoughts, which create your emotions, which evolve into your actions and words. Your words then reinforce your beliefs and the cycle continues.

I want you to really think about this concept, because it's really freaking important. Your beliefs, values, self-image and worldview are all organized inside your mind and ready to turn into thoughts to narrate the things that you see and experience. Your thoughts then make you feel a certain kind of way, because emotions naturally come as a result of our thoughts. And now your emotions then lead to words (speaking something) or an action (doing something). Your actions will reinforce your beliefs, and thus repeat the cycle. This is simply because your brain wants to constantly prove that the belief system is correct. Therefore it will delete and distort any information that goes against what it currently believes to be true.

Let's circle back to habits to get a clearer understanding of all of this. Your habits are stored in the oldest part of your brain: the reptilian part. The reptilian part of the brain is concerned mainly with just survival. It doesn't distinguish between good and bad habits. All habits are just habits. We have habits that facilitate our daily tasks without the need to relearn them every time. Think about it like this: see how you're reading these words right now? You're not sounding out each letter like you did when you were first learning your phonics. You're just...reading.

This is your subconscious mind at work. You walk, talk, drive, and brush your teeth, all without consciously thinking about it. You don't have to relearn everything every time you do it. It would be exhausting to have to think through absolutely everything we do every time we do it. So, in this sense, our subconscious minds are actually a gift. In some ways, it makes our lives a heck of a lot easier. I'm seriously so glad I don't have to relearn how to read and write every time I sit down to write another chapter. I would be stressed to the max if I had to be consciously aware of everything that I was doing at one time. So let's give a big round of applause to our subconscious minds for being the real OG. Being able to retain knowledge, and then retrieve it when we need it is real badass.

However, there is still a pretty big issue that we will run into with our submind. What do we do when we're misinformed and are believing lies? Is there a way to help our sub-minds relearn what they have already stored, or is it too late and we're just stuck this way?

I'm glad you asked, because that's exactly what I'm here to teach you. We'll dive deeper into this in the next chapters, but for now I want you to know that any belief, habit or thought that is stored within your mind can be changed, released and replaced with the truth. Our brains are pretty freaking amazing, and once you learn how to harness the abilities of your subconscious mind, you're in for a whole lot of abundance, success, and love.

So what the heck do we do then? How do we start? We start by becoming wildly aware of what it is that we believe to be true, so that we can stop the vicious cycle of letting our subconscious mind determine what is or isn't good for us. It's time to take back control of your mind and become the one and only one that chooses your reality. And that, my friend, is the process of becoming the author of your life.

Chapter Four/

The Observer

"You have power over your mind— not outside events. Realize this, and you will find strength." -Marcus Aurelius

What is a thought? Stop for a second and think about what a thought is. That might sound like a ridiculous thing to do— to think about what a thought is. But do it with me anyway. We have thoughts all day long. If you are like me, you may have constant dialogue with yourself going on in your mind all day long. Reasoning with yourself, ruminating on things that have happened in the past, hypothesizing on things that may happen in the future, and narrating to yourself about things that are currently happening to you in the present. Your thoughts can be really fucking powerful, and I'm sure, more than once in your life, you've talked yourself into what I like to call, a hurricane thought spiral. This happens when you have overthought about something until you were sure that people hated you, that you messed up or that your worth is determined by something trivial.

When I was in the depths of my anxiety and eating disorder, I realized it was all heightened by my thoughts. And that thought hurricane spiral? It was pretty wild. It would start with a simple thought about how I looked, and then after a million terrible additional thoughts, I would be crying under my blankets, not wanting anyone to see me. If you are alone with these types of thoughts long enough, they can absolutely deteriorate your self confidence. You will begin to believe things about yourself that are not true, and slowly limit yourself to only things that you think you deserve. You miss career opportunities because you don't think you are qualified. You don't allow yourself to be fully loved because you believe that you've messed up too badly to love again. The list can go on, but are you beginning to see how powerful your thoughts are? You can back yourself into an imaginary corner by the things that you believe about yourself that aren't even true.

Something I talk about with my clients is that everything is inherently neutral. We have the power to make it mean whatever we want. The same goes for your thoughts, meaning that they in themselves are not inherently good or bad. They are just notions that pass through our conscious and subconscious minds. The issues develop when we believe these thoughts, attach ourselves to them, begin to identify ourselves by them or allow them to dictate our actions. You can dismiss or entertain thoughts, and this is how you can give thoughts their power.

Merriam-Webster has many different definitions for the word, but the one I want to hone in on is this:

"Thought, something (such as an opinion or belief) in the mind"

So, a thought is just an opinion or belief in your mind. It's neutral. Not necessarily true, just an opinion or belief in your mind. You can take it or leave it, believe it or dismiss it, it's totally up to you. However, the thoughts you may be experiencing are most often negative and unless we are consistently practicing mindfulness and learning to listen to the spirit, then the majority of thoughts that you entertain are going to be from the ego and are going to be negative thoughts. And over time, listening to negative thought after negative thought, you begin to believe them.

Think about how many times you've talked yourself into a bad mood versus the number of times you've talked yourself into a good mood. The ratio probably doesn't look too good, but I want to make it extremely clear—you have the ability to talk yourself into a good mood too! And you do it just exactly how you talk yourself into a bad one. You can choose to listen to the positive thoughts about yourself instead of listening to the negative ones. All it takes is practice. It's called neuroplasticity and it's possible for you! Consistently observing the thoughts and redirecting them or reframing them without judgment creates new learned behavioral thoughts. Let me also be very super clear about this, intrusive thoughts will always pop up even after you do mindset training, but you will never react the same way as you do now.

Here's a simple illustration for you. Right now, I have a labradoodle in my backyard and she's hanging out under the picnic table. It's a warm summer's day, and my initial thought is that she's sad and lonely because I'm not out there playing fetch with her. If I entertain this thought, it could take me to some crazy places. I could end up thinking that I'm a bad dog mom. Maybe I don't give her enough attention. Maybe I should rehome her to someone that can give her more love than I can! As I am thinking all of these things, my pup is probably perfectly happy. She is thinking about all the yummy food I just gave her for breakfast as she watches the birds and squirrels run around her yard.

Our thoughts are not reality, they are our perception of life based on our inner thought world. Just because I see my dog sitting alone and automatically think she's sad doesn't mean that she actually is sad. The exact opposite could be true, but I've already attached my belief to the negative thought before the positive thought ever had the chance to cross my mind. I'd already convinced myself of something and all I did was look outside and observe my dog. I'd made myself feel guilty over literally nothing, and this same principle can apply to whatever we find ourselves observing. Your friend isn't as chatty as she usually is, so you assume you've done something wrong when maybe she's just hungry or had a long morning. I can go on with examples, but I think you know exactly what I'm talking about.

Thoughts, on their own, cannot cause either our happiness or our unhappiness. They are just that: thoughts. It is only when we hear those thoughts and choose to listen and embrace them that we either stumble or stand. Instead of attaching to a thought, what do we do with them? We should simply notice them. Watch and observe your thoughts as they pass through your mind. In the beginning, as you learn to observe your thoughts as an outsider, it might help to write them down. Seeing a thought written on paper can help you identify really quickly whether or not a thought is an illusion or the truth. Somehow, when a thought is all locked away inside your mind, it seems a lot more true and convincing than it really is. Write it down. Does it seem like a possible illusion now? It probably is. Now scribble that out and write the truth down or what you would like to believe instead, and repeat that truth to yourself in place of the illusion.

I'm not a bad dog mom. Scratch that. I'm a good dog mom and I treat her well. She has a better life than I do some days! She has a family that loves her, a huge yard to play in, food and water, endless balls and toys to play with, squirrels and bunnies to chase. I take her on walks in nature. I make sure she's healthy by keeping up with her vet visits. I give her treats for being a good girl. My dog is LOVED and she loves me too.

NOTICE thoughts instead of investing and attaching to them. Look at all the thoughts that you have and choose to believe only the ones that serve you. Slow down and listen to the spirit within you. What is true and what is just an illusion that keeps popping up in your mind? Dismiss the lie. Literally say out loud "*I DISMISS THIS THOUGHT. IT IS A LIE.*" And then focus your attention elsewhere. Replace the lies with truth and only dwell on the truth. The most important thing you can do is practice this and ensure you observe the thoughts and take action before they do the hurricane spiral into affecting your nervous system.

Entertaining thoughts reinforces them for our minds. That's how we get into trouble when we start bottling things up and overthinking. We start to believe our thoughts because we keep reinforcing them and repeating them to ourselves over and over. After a while, we begin to believe them. We start to think that...maybe..they are true...

The cool thing is, this works the exact same way when we choose to reinforce the truth and to entertain positive and uplifting thoughts. We can put ourselves into a good headspace by "overthinking" about positive thoughts and the things that the spirit brings to our minds. We start to believe them because we keep reinforcing them and repeating them to ourselves over and over. After a while, we begin to believe what is true. Sound familiar? This is how our minds work. And when you learn this, you can transform your life and recreate it into the life that you want it to be, all by learning which thoughts to throw out and which ones to entertain.

Thoughts are just a vapor; one appears just as another disappears. They come and go and you should let them do so. Let them come, and let them go just as easily. They have no power over you, they're just little bits of narrative that have no authority or entitlement to a place in your mind. You're the fucking queen of your mind— you and you only get to choose which thoughts go and which ones stay. In fact, YOU hold the power, and here is how I can show you. Let's play a game, shall we? Close your eyes for a moment and say in your head, "*I love you!*" Did you hear that? Now say it again but louder, "*I LOVE YOU!*" And now one more time, yell as loudly in your head as you can, "*I FREAKING LOVE YOU!!*" That my friend was all you. You created the thought, heard it, and then controlled its volume. Pretty cool, right? That's the queen right there, in control and in her power.

Now all of this being said, though it is true, there is still something I want to point out. Negative thoughts are the most easily believed and that's because your brain tends to focus on the negative ones in order to ensure your safety. I've said it before, but your subconscious is concerned with protecting you. So, when a negative thought pops up, alarms go off because your brain wants to make sure nothing bad happens to you. And in some cases, this is a very good thing. There are some negative thoughts that are true. You can find yourself stuck in a toxic situation or relationship if you choose to ignore all of the negative thoughts that pass through your mind. That's why mindfulness is so important. You have to be still long enough to hear the truth from the spirit. And sometimes, the truth is that your friend really is toxic and it would be better for your mental health if you put some boundaries on that relationship or walked away completely. It's a fine line, but if you want to cultivate a growth mindset, it has to be done on purpose and with great intention.

Weigh your thoughts, dismiss the lies, but don't fall into toxic positivity. Learn to listen with wisdom so that you can discern what is TRUE and choose to believe and embrace that.

Here are some ways I help guide my clients to view their thoughts differently.

Knowing that your ego generally speaks negatively, we want to imagine the ego as a separate person. Think of this person maybe as a small child who is scared and needs security and safety. I want you to think of those intrusive or negative thoughts coming from that scared child. Now with that visual, you can step up to the plate and re-parent her with love the way she always needed. Hear the thoughts, and instead of punishing the small child, imagine them deeply craving to be accepted and loved. This will allow you to switch to empathy and caring when reframing thoughts.

If you are a visual kinda gal, I want you to try out this activity. You can use a picture of yourself when you were a child, or if you are a momma, you can use a picture of your child. Grab a photo of yourself (or child) when you were between the ages of 0-12. Keep it with you and when an intrusive thought comes up, pull out the photo and look at her. Tell her, "*I love you exactly as you are; you are safe.*" Reparenting your little you will allow you to release the things that you are blaming yourself for that were not your fault, and to embrace the parts of you that so desperately needed acceptance.

Another thing you can do is called "The Rooted Why." When you are feeling stuck with resistance when pursuing a goal or showing up in your business, ask yourself, "*What am I afraid is going to happen?*" Your little you will search in the depths of the subconscious for an answer. Be patient because, though you could receive an answer immediately, it can take up to a couple days to hear an answer. When you hear the answer, trust the answer and then ask why. You will then get a new answer and ask why again. Ask why a total of 5 times and you will get your deeper resistance revealed.

From there, you will ask yourself,
Do I believe this to be 100% true?
Who taught me this?
Is this MY story or theirs?
Can I give myself permission to release it?
What would I like to believe instead?

It is then imperative that you do not judge these answers. They are simply things you have been taught by past experiences, stories of the people who raised you and societal expectations and NONE of that is your fault. Ever.

I'd love to share with you an example I made for myself about 5 years ago before I healed my money story.

I first had to ask myself why I was feeling resistance. The answer was that I was feeling resistance when trying to make more money.

So I asked myself, why?

"I am afraid of what people will think of me."

Why?

"I am afraid they will think I am better than them."

Why?

"Because I've always struggled with making more money."

Why?

"Because I was taught that the more money you make, the more greedy you are."

Who taught you this?

"My parents."

And is that your story or theirs?

"Theirs."

Can I give myself the permission to release this story and create my own?

"*YES!*"

What would I like to believe instead?

"*I get to decide how easy it will be! As long as I am doing the work that lights me up, money is the byproduct of that!*"

Become the author and write your new story! Making more money doesn't have to be hard and is simply an amplifier of the good inside of you. The ones who love you will love you no matter what. Making more money will bring you so much less stress, more fulfilling experiences, and the ability to help so many people. Your success will create a ripple effect of good!

Follow this outline for the resistance that you are feeling.

1. Where is it coming from?

2. Why?

3. Where did you learn this?

4. Is it your story, or does that story belong to someone else?

And give yourself permission to release their story and to write your own. You don't have to live in someone else's story or be boxed in by someone else's limitations. You're a free freaking goddess. Now go create your own reality!

Chapter Five/
Healing the Little You

"Your inner child gets it all, believes it all, hopes for it all... That child knows that life—which runs on love and feasts on creativity—is on your side..." -Andrea Balt

I recently saw a TikTok trend in which you sit down, close your eyes, and imagine receiving a hug from your little kid self. Imagine telling your younger self all about what you have accomplished and the dreams that you once had that you are now living in. Really sit in the moment and consider how far you have come, and imagine what your younger self would say had she known all that you would go on to accomplish. I bet you would make yourself proud. I know I am freaking proud of who I have grown to be and I want the same for you, too.

We all have an inner child within us and when we get triggered by something in our life, this always relates to a young, unhealed part within ourselves. Your inner child is your original or true self and by doing intentional healing, you are coming back home to yourself and remembering the brilliance that was always there.

We have all had different childhood experiences, but one consistent thing that we have all experienced to some degree is childhood trauma. Not exclusively physical trauma, though that could be a part of it, but also mental, emotional and spiritual trauma. When we experience this trauma as a child, the part of us that was hurt becomes stuck and unable to age and mature naturally. Whether we experience anger, physical pain, or maybe sadness because of an experience, a defense mechanism builds up within the subconscious mind to protect us from that situation ever repeating itself. Your subconscious mind then forms a wounded inner child.

As we grow and mature into adults, there can be things that trigger those childhood traumas, and they can take your mind back to re-experience those things. Most of our subconscious minds will have grown and matured along with our physical bodies, but since that wounded part of your subconscious mind has been frozen in time, when these traumas are brought back up, you will respond with your inner child and the level of maturity that you possessed when you first experienced that trauma.

Maybe you had strict parents growing up that were hard on you for good grades, or a mom that had an eating disorder that you have now taken on. And now your inner child finds its value in the things that you accomplish or the people that you please or the way that you look and how healthy you eat. Until we work through these traumas and learn to rework our subconscious minds to release the illusions and the stories of others that have been stored as truth within our subconscious minds, we are an adult with pieces of our subconscious that are stuck in our childhood.

You could have several wounded inner children within you, depending on the trauma that you experienced and what ages you were when you experienced each of those. And it is possible to be triggered over and over again by those past traumas and that is what will likely happen until you are able to identify and work through each of them. It is also possible to have trauma that creates an inner child in your teens, twenties and beyond. They are younger wounded versions of you stored within your subconscious.

Our tendency may be to eliminate the triggers. Asking for a raise is a trigger, so avoid it. Applying for your dream job is a trigger, so avoid it. However, the triggers, you see, are not the issue. In fact, the triggers are your teachers that will shed light on what is going on within your subconscious mind and give you the opportunity to learn and heal from these traumas that you are unknowingly holding onto. When you approach the trigger with compassion and curiosity instead of wounded energy, you will see this is a message and a plea for help from your small inner child. Your inner child may be disguised by inner resistance, fear, sadness, hopelessness, etc. And this inner child needs to be met, not with critical or judgemental thoughts, but with reassurance and comfort.

Your wounded inner child deeply craves the support and unconditional love from you, the adult version of you, just like a child would long for the approval and love from an empowered parent. Instead of giving the power to your wounded inner child, you can learn to step into your empowered divine energy, love your inner child and release the years of pain that you have been holding on to.

Why is it so important to heal your inner child? I have a friend that is one of the most talented creatives that I know, but she has never been able to see her work in its greatness. She began working on her art in her young teen years and received critical feedback about her work that she took to heart and damaged her view of her talents. She is now one of the most talented creatives in her local art industry and she is still afraid to apply for projects or charge her worth because her wounded inner child is still stuck in those teenage years. Hearing those discouraging comments about her work way back in her younger years is still holding her back from working and networking with other creatives that are also creating at her level of expertise.

When you get stuck in these spots, you are allowing your inner child to dictate your future out of fear and self-preservation. You don't want to hear critical thoughts about your work. You don't want someone to be disappointed in you. You don't want to experience those emotions again, so you steer clear of situations that may bring those emotions back up.

Can you see why healing your inner child is so important? There are things that you have been holding on to from your younger years that are still wreaking havoc on your current life goals. And since these are all held within your subconscious, you are likely not yet aware of them.

Your triggers are your teacher to show you what things you are still stuck and afraid of. These triggers can show up as being a people pleaser and not being able to stick to your boundaries. It can show up as being an overachiever or workaholic because you want to prove your worth to everyone around you. Or it can show up as withdrawing from your surroundings or removing yourself entirely from a difficult situation instead of facing it head on.

So what do we do about these inner children within? Become wildly aware. That's our motto. Recognize when you are feeling resistance or when your peace is being disrupted. Once you recognize a feeling, thought, or action that is triggering you, you can ask whether that is coming from a place of truth or a lie, ego or the spirit. Once you can see how your inner child is reaching out, you can learn to build a bridge between your adult self and your inner child to create a new narrative about the situation that you are experiencing.

I use energetics to help support my community as a form of growth and development. Within energetics, there are both masculine and feminine energies. There is also a wounded and healed version of these energies. The healed versions of these energies are called: divine masculine and divine feminine energy. You can find both masculine and feminine energy within us all. I'm not talking about gender or sexuality, I'm referring to energy. Every person is going to have varying levels of both masculine and feminine energy, but ideally, there should be a healthy balance between the two.

So what are these energies and how do they show up in your life? Well, whenever you find feelings of struggling with low self worth, constant comparison, weak boundaries, trouble saying no, feeling bad when we do set boundaries, etc. These are examples of wounded feminine energy. These feelings and beliefs can usually be traced back to the feminine energies that influenced your life between the ages of 0-12. This could be a grandmother, mother, foster parents, etc. It could have even been your dad or a male figure as well. Think about who it was in your life that was the feminine energy.

Usually, when we are in wounded energies, we are embodying the energy of those who raised us or the emotional energetic abandonment of a particular female or masculine energy. In my life, my mother was the feminine energy that helped form my beliefs around feminine energy. Let me be super clear, my mother is flippin' magical. I do not cast blame or judgment on how she raised me. My mother raised me with immense love and she did the best she could with the tools she had at that time. However, growing up, I took on her wounded feminine energy and began to live in that. It wasn't until I forgave that version of her and saw her with eyes of love and began my own healing that I was able to let go of my own wounded feminine and step into the divine feminine that was waiting for me. I recognized, released, and stepped into the divine energy. That's exactly what I want for you, too.

Maybe you were abandoned by a feminine energy, maybe you took on the feminine energy that you were raised with, maybe you never had a strong feminine energy in your life and you feel resentment toward that energy. Whatever your story, it is so important to pinpoint where your wounded feminine is coming from so that you can release it.

Wounded masculine can look like forcefulness, distrust that the universe or divine is going to provide for you. It could look like overworking, being busy-minded, or being over competitive. If you are experiencing any of these, then you need to think about the wounded masculine energy that you are experiencing. Who represented that masculine during your childhood? Where did the wounded masculine energy within you originate?

Healthy masculine energy can be described as freedom, purpose, mission, liberation, creating solutions, structure, strategy, achievement, success. Masculine energy stands in strength. It is not overly controlling or dominant, forceful or aggressive. It is open, focused, and strong.

Feminine energy is the heart flow of the energies. It is the feeling, emotion, intuition, creation, expression, radiance.

This is feminine energy in the divine sense. This is what healthy feminine energy looks like in your life. For me, I had both traits of wounded masculine and wounded feminine, so, I began releasing control, leaning into faith, and allowing more play and creative expression.

When you learn to heal the masculine and feminine, it is then that you will be in balance and alignment and able to make decisions and move forward in whatever your goals are for your life. If you're struggling with those feelings of low self-esteem, comparison, or setting boundaries, etc. This is the wounded feminine energies that are showing up within your inner child.

So where do we start? You start by reparenting your inner child. Meeting your inner child where they are, creating an open dialogue, and asking questions to begin to uncover the source of the wounds. You can do things like meditating and listening, writing a letter to your inner child to cultivate dialogue and set aside time to simply feel what it is that is going on inside of you.

I used to be so afraid of feeling feelings that I simply avoided them by overworking, too much alcohol consumption, and never being still. Once I approached healing with a sense of curiosity, the more it felt like I was just finding all the pieces of my past and making sense of where they came from. I observed them without judgment and allowed myself to move through each piece on its own. This way, it didn't feel overwhelming, it felt intentional and, for the first time, healing felt possible. Approaching healing your inner child with a sense of childlike curiosity can be an excellent start toward reparenting your little you.

Here are 3 journal prompts to start with:

1. As a child, what did you not get enough of?

2. How can you provide love and care for your inner-child?

3. If you had to say something to your inner child right now, what would you say?

Meditation is going to be your best friend through this process. Meditation is a learned habit that allows you to hear how busy your mind is and how trapped your thoughts are. It's the practice of hearing thoughts, and always ushering yourself back to the present still moment. I've heard this so many times, "*I can't meditate!*" I would ask you to unpack that statement a little. If you believe slowing your mind down will be hard or you can't do it, that is the story you will believe. If you open yourself to curiosity and try to start to allow yourself to notice the narrative in your mind, you will notice your thoughts rolling through. Observe them, notice them, experience them and then let them float by. Listen, be still, and notice. My best advice is to not attach good or bad notions to the thoughts. And one more thing, feel the feelings. This is how we move through things and heal from them. And I promise you will soon realize that feeling is nothing to be scared of.

When we allow our thoughts to take over by dismissing them or not giving them thought, we allow them to take our power from us. You can begin to take your power back by saying yes to yourself. Maybe that looks like going on a hike, playing your favorite music and having a solo dance off. Whatever choosing yourself looks like, choose it. Choose whatever it is that allows yourself to experience more love and attention while you are navigating the thoughts of your inner narrative.

As you are working to reconnect with your inner child, do things that you did back then. Did you like to play? Paint? Draw? What toy or book did you always want as a child that you were disappointed you never got? Find a freaking Polly Pocket, Furby, jelly sandals or lip smackers chapstick, whatever it was, and buy it. Begin to connect again with your inner child and show that you care, that you're available and you are ready to listen.

Why is ALL OF THIS important? Because we manifest from our level of perceived worthiness. You will only manifest from how healed your inner child is and how healed your subconscious mind is. If your little you is not healed enough, you will most likely sabotage receiving the good you crave.

Sit with yourself. Put on some meditative music or hertz frequencies off of a streaming service and give yourself a couple minutes to simply be still and listen to the voice of your inner child. If it helps, grab a photo of yourself as a child and hold space for them as you start to dive into the discovery of you. And most importantly, be patient and kind with yourself in the process.

Chapter Six/
The Attractor

"Choose your thoughts carefully. You are the masterpiece of your life." -Rhonda Byrne

Girl, you're electric. For real. Your body literally has an electric field. Anywhere within you that has a nerve, also has an electric current. Have you ever touched someone and shocked them? That's just a small example of the energy within you. Your brain has electric wave patterns and they work just like the light of the stars, the electromagnetic spectrum, and it is within this electric energy that your thoughts are formed.

Some of the brain waves that are surging energy and electricity in your brain are the thoughts that are bouncing around in your head right now as you read this chapter. As you read the words, there is understanding and processing that is going on. These thoughts are pure energy. And this energy is subject to the same rules that all energy is subjected to. The Law of Attraction, the way your neurons work, it all works the same way. When you begin to understand a little science behind electricity and energy, you will also begin to understand how to manifest the life you deeply crave and desire.

But let's take a few baby steps first. The one way that we are different from the light of the stars and the electrical current of an electron is that we are conscious beings with the ability to choose and think freely. We have a will and we aren't just subject to whatever may happen to us. We can choose how things affect us, and how we want to respond, therefore giving us the full power to become the author of our own lives. The way that we do this is by choosing new thoughts. Our minds are, in essence, transmitters that are able to send and receive signals from the universe around us. The signals that we are sending with our thoughts, words, emotions and actions are the signals that are going to shape our reality.

Your thoughts create your life. The way that you think about yourself, your worth, ability, talent, and destiny are all shaping your future. That may sound a little intense right now, but hear me out. Remember how we said earlier that our brains are receptors? That means that your thoughts don't just stay within your head. The words that you speak don't just disappear and fly away with the wind. Your emotions aren't felt by only you and then simply dissipate. All of these things hold tremendous energy, and that energy goes into the universe and will send back whatever experience matches that energetic vibration. Every thought you entertain sends a signal. Every word you speak, another signal is sent. Every action, emotion, thought, signal, signal, signal. Are you beginning to see it? We are constantly, whether we are aware of it or not, sending signals into the universe.

So what's the big deal? Why does that matter? It matters because of the Law of Attraction. The Law of Attraction, simply stated, is that like attracts like. Whatever you are thinking, whatever you are believing, feeling, saying, doing, etc. When we put our energy into the universe, since like attracts like, we are attracting more of that same energy back to ourselves. This is how your thoughts create your life. And this is why it is so important for you to become wildly aware of what it is that you are entertaining.

Here's a simple example of how thoughts become things.Think of a building right now, maybe your house. Your house didn't just appear one day. Boom, a house. Before your house existed, it first existed in the mind of an architect. Your house was built first in someone's mind. Then it was created. Everything is created twice, once by thought and then by creation.

Have you ever really really wanted something, but didn't think you could ever get it? Maybe there's a car that you dream about, or a house in the community that you would love to have. You've seen these things, and you wish that you had them, but you know that it would never be possible. They cost too much, and you've resolved in your mind that you won't ever be able to live that kind of lifestyle. According to the Law of Attraction, you can get anything you want. It doesn't matter how much things cost, or how far out of your lifestyle budget they seem, since everything you want is just energy.

So if you're made up of energy, and everything you want is made up of energy, you can attract that life you crave and bring it into existence if you can just learn how to attract it. At this point, you may be either excited or doubtful, but here is what I'd like you to consider: you are already manifesting. The concept I am diving into is called intentional manifesting. Say this out loud, *"SHOW ME HOW THIS CAN BE EASY!"* I say this all of the damn time and guess what? The intention of ease always shows the way. So let's see how manifesting the life you desire can be easy, and maybe even delicious and fun! The way that you attract your life's cravings is by taking hold of your thoughts, words, beliefs, emotions and actions and becoming wildly aware of them. They are all manifesting your current life! Look around you. What do you see? You see exactly what you have manifested for yourself. The life that you have is the energy that you have been putting out. YOU have created the life that you have, whether you realize that or not. If there is something you want to change, you can. If there is something you want to create, you can. The moment you choose yourself, is the moment you take action towards creating the life you crave. The moment you decide to heal, forgive, write your own story, own your power, then the magic unfolds.

Another thing you need to be aware of is Hebb's Law. Hebb's Law states that nerves that fire together, wire together. We talked about our thoughts in previous chapters, but I want to dive in a little deeper now into understanding the science behind it all.

It will help to think of the mind like a map. Over the course of your lifetime, your brain has been busy working. Maybe you haven't consciously noticed it, but your brain has taken all of the external stimuli that you have experienced and stored it, neatly organized, within your mind. Whether it be taste, smell, emotions, touch, or memories, your brain has stored them and has also stored them in relation to other things that we experienced at the same time. This is your neural networking at play.

Let's say, for example, you touched a hot stove. Immediately, you felt a physical pain that was correlated with touching the hot surface of your stove. Since you felt pain as you touched the surface, your brain scooped up those two experiences and stored them in connection with each other. Now the pain and the hot surface have been fused together and stored within your mind for future retrieval. Next time you see a hot stove, you won't have to touch it to remember the physical pain that it can cause.

In this instance, other emotions could also have been correlated to the hot stove. If a baby touched the stove, they might now feel fear when seeing the stove again. This is what is called Hebb's Law. *"Neurons that fire together wire together."* Hot stove, physical pain, and fear. They all occurred together because of one experience and now those neurons will fire together in the future because they have now been wired together. Within your brain, there are millions of neurons that are firing together because of all of the millions of different things that you have experienced within your life and you may not even be aware of any of them.

Why does this even matter? Good question. There are times in our lives when our brains wire things together that shouldn't necessarily be correlated. Some correlations are good. When I am thinking of my husband, I think of his strong hugs, his constant whistling, and eclectic music. All of those things are good and true. But sometimes, your brain wires things together that shouldn't be together.

Someone who watched their mother go through a toxic relationship could have negative thoughts attached to love, commitment, or just romantic relationships in general. Your mom experienced fear, pain, and emotional turmoil in correlation with love, but that doesn't mean that every single relationship is that way. Unfortunately, your brain doesn't understand all of that. All you see is love and pain connected. And they stay that way in your brain and it ends up affecting the way that you engage in future relationships. These are neurons within your brain that have been fused together in the past that now fire together in present and future circumstances.

This is the first thing that I want you to become wildly aware of: are there things in your life that have been fused together from a past experience that is now affecting current circumstances? These not-so-great connections can result in self-sabotage and if we are going to take our power back, live intentionally, and become the author of our own lives, then we have some work to do.

So, step 1? Same thing we keep saying. Become wildly aware! What thoughts are floating around in your mind? Grab them, write them down. Where are they coming from? Do you find yourself talking negatively to yourself all day? Why do you do that? Is it because of neurons that have fused together that shouldn't have? Maybe there is some neural networking that you need to work on rewiring. Maybe you have a metaphorical stove top that you need to touch, but the fear and pain that is associated with it from that one hot stove is holding you back.

Yours probably isn't a literal stove top. Maybe it's slowing down at work, going back to school for more training, talking to your friend about setting some relational boundaries, or even taking the next step in your romantic relationship. Something is holding you back from just freaking diving in and doing it. What is causing that resistance?

Ask yourself why. Why do you find it so hard to set boundaries? Maybe because you feel bad. Why does that make you feel bad? The more you ask yourself why you will start to discover a younger you who may have been hurt. Boom, inner child located. Time to reparent and love that inner child and teach your subconscious mind that boundaries are good! They are necessary for your mental sanity, and your anxiety around boundaries is just neural networking that needs a little rewiring and love.

The next thing I want you to be aware of is word association and the power of the "I AM" statement. Want to know something crazy? Every single word in your vocabulary holds memory and emotion, therefore you will have a rush of feelings every time you speak. Here's an example: I love coffee, like, really love coffee. So just the word coffee gives me a warm and happy feeling in my body. But what if you hated coffee? You can imagine how you might not have the same reaction as me. What about the word boundaries? If I associate the word boundaries with confrontation, and I fear confrontation, just the word boundary will make me feel nervous. And once your fear center in your mind is activated by your nervousness, it will amp up the scary thoughts and feelings to ensure you move to safety. Here is something I teach my students: swap the word that feels heavy for something more empowering and notice how it immediately changes how you feel.

"I AM" is a statement of creation. Anything that you say after "I AM" begins the creation of that statement. Isn't that so powerful?! So, if we want to change your disempowering beliefs, you must reverse engineer by changing your words. But here is the most important thing: you must be in harmony with your subconscious mind before you start using any kind of affirmation. If you're not in harmony with your submind, then it won't trust you, and will call your bluff.

Harmony with your submind + realistic, emotionally infused positive affirmation + inspired action = rewiring your brain.

Your words are the number one most powerful way to reinforce your belief system. What you say is what you get, every single time. Your belief lives at the core of your submind, and from your belief system comes your thoughts, then feelings, then words and actions. Whatever words you speak are then reinforced your belief system. It's a constant cycle, and the only way that we can break out of the cycle is to work backwards and flip your script.

"I AM" is a statement of creation. Think of this as your magic button to get whatever it is that you want. Everything you start saying "I AM" before is actually going to create that for you. Think back, now, to all the things you've spoken into existence with your "I AM" statements.

"I am broke."

"I am not good enough."

"I am unworthy."

"I am bad with money."

If these are all you've ever spoken to yourself, then your current life may be starting to make more sense. When you can get on the other side of the power of "I AM" and begin to use this to speak good things, and to begin to create the reality of abundance that you want.

When you start consciously using "I AM" statements, your life will begin to transform. This isn't something that only works for the lucky people, this is something that works for EVERYONE. But it is going to take intentional work and practice. After you have practiced this consciously, it will become an unconscious habit over time, and you will have trained your mind to create good and bring it to your life. After time, this will simply be your way of operating.

Let's speak your "I AM" truths. These are your affirmations. The things that may not be true right this second, but that your brain needs to start believing so that we can start making them happen.

I AM exactly the person to do this.

I AM smart.

I AM brave.

I AM a successful business woman.

I AM deserving of happiness and love.

If your brain immediately calls bullshit, here is an activity you can try instead. See how it opens up your mind to the light of possibility!

What if I was exactly the person to do this?

What if I was always smart?

What if I was brave?

What if I was a successful business woman?

What if I was deserving of happiness and love?

Write down your "I AM" statements or "What If" statements. They are life-giving. They are creating energy that is going to attract like energy. Get a pen and paper and write them down. Speak them out loud, and with some damn hype! Remember, we need that high vibe energy to infuse these and activate Hebb's Law. And yes, speak them out loud! This is very important since your voice is one of the most important vibrations for massive energy change.

Essentially, you need to convince your brain that something that has not yet happened is already true. So, then your brain can begin to send out those attractive signals so that you can manifest those things. Everything that you THINK creates a FEELING in your body. That feeling is conscious awareness and it's you being aware of the energy that you are in.

"I'll never be good enough to (XYZ)."

First off, YES YOU ARE. Second, when we become the author of our lives, we now get the power to choose. Choose new thoughts, new beliefs, and new creations for our lives.

Everything is only two things:

The presence of what you want, or the absence of what you want.

You attract the circumstances that MATCH your energy.

On a physiological level, you are sending a signal of lack to your subconscious mind, and your mind picks up that energy and then starts to recreate that experience over and over again.

So let's create the energy of a damn goddess, ready?

Instead of, "w*hat if I SUCK at this?*"

We can choose to think, "w*hat if I do really well at this?*"

Instead of, "*what if people judge me?*"

We can choose to think, "*what if I find joy and help people?*"

Instead of, "*what if no one likes me?*"

We can choose to think, "w*hat if I fall in love with myself?*"

Instead of, "*what will people think?*"

We can choose to think, "*will this give me fulfillment?*"

Instead of, "*who am I to become wealthy?!?*"

We can choose to think, "*being wealthy is the best! The amount of income I have is a direct result of all of the people I've helped! And I can help myself and so many others by being wealthy!*"

Instead of, "*WHAT IF I FAIL?!?*"

We can choose to think, "*What If I fucking SOAR?*"

This is all neuroscience, and we are about to become experts on how to tell our brains what to think. You know how things can accidentally fuse together in your brain? Well, all you have to do is follow the rules and you can start INTENTIONALLY wiring these neurons together. I'm a super visual learner and I remember in 8th grade biology, I had to memorize all the parts of the cell for an exam. I knew there was absolutely no way I was actually going to be able to memorize all those parts. So ya know what I did? I connected every part to a color or adjective. The maroon mitochondria, the violet vacuoles, the gnarly nucleus (I know, it doesn't start with an N..) and what do you know? Aced the test. Was it because I was super awesome at memorization? No, it's because I was fusing some neurons together so that when I got into that test, those neurons would fire together.

What do you need to start firing together? Do you have negative emotions that are connected to good things that you want for your life? Maybe you need to start rewiring some neural networking within your brain so that you can start manifesting the life that you want. It all starts with becoming wildly aware of your life creating thoughts, the things you're feeling resistance to, and the words that you allow to come out of your mouth. It's time to dig deep.

Buckle up and start journaling your way through this. Write down your negative thoughts that are holding you back. Identify where they are coming from and recreate those thoughts as positive I AM statements to start putting truth back into the universe.

You've got this.

And while you do this you should also be listening to this song:

LIZZO - Like A Girl

(You're welcome.)

Chapter Seven/
The Beautiful Rebuild

"Healing may not be so much about getting better, as about letting go of everything that isn't you— all of the expectations, all of the beliefs—and becoming who you are." -Rachel Naomi Remen

Okay my friend. Up until this point, I have shared all about healing, understanding the science behind our subconscious mind, the influence that our thoughts have over our lives and reworking some of the illusions and misconceptions that we have been holding on to. But here's the deal, I want to help you rebuild all of those areas that you've been breaking down barriers in. I don't want you to just smother them with things you think you should say, I want you to replace them with truth and light. I want to ensure that you have rebuilt your relationship with all aspects of your life and your business so that we can then begin to intentionally manifest the life that you've been dreaming of.

If you want more good in your life, you need to make some damn space for it! This means taking an energy audit on all things. This includes your habits, the people in your life, and digging even deeper into what you believe about your worthiness, your self confidence and your relationship with money and receiving it. Excuses are out, procrastination is out. We're here, right now, and we're going to do this dang thing. We are now embodying powerful goddess energy and what does a powerful goddess do? She takes full accountability and responsibility for her life. She is the mother effin' author. She writes the story, she chooses her energy wisely and she invests in the right people. So let's get started, shall we?

YOUR HABITS

Want to know something wild? You have 65,000 - 75,000 thoughts that pop into your mind every single day. 95% of those thoughts are recycled from the previous day, and the day before that, and the day before that, and 70% of them are negative. This results in the same feelings, behaviors, and habits every day, which then result in the same manifestations within your life.

When you think about your thoughts like this, it makes a lot of sense that you keep manifesting the same things back into your life over and over. When you want to change the way or the things that you are manifesting, the key is to start with your thoughts. Your thoughts carry emotions, which results in actions and eventually your words and how you show up in the world.

When I was deep in my eating disorder, I would wake up morning after morning with the exact same thought that would arise. *"How much did I eat yesterday?"* If my perception of a small amount was met, I would have a feeling of worthiness rush over my brain and then allow me to continue feeling that only until I looked at my body. If my wounded perception agreed with the visual, I could continue feeling worthy. However, if I thought I had eaten too much the day prior, my first thought process was, *"you have no self control, you piece of shit."* That negative narrative would continue and distort the view of my body, how my clothes felt, and how I thought others must see me, too.

Changing your thoughts and habits may sound impossible and even heart wrenching, but it is actually something that you can do immediately and that you have full control over. The moment I became wildly aware of my thoughts, I understood that if I continued to attach myself to them, I would continue feeling the same feelings again and again. It has to come to a point where you have your *"I'm fucking done"* moment. The moment where your current thought processes or life experiences are too painful to continue and you deeply crave relief. Redirecting and shifting your habitual thought patterns is going to allow you to build worthiness and strength, to allow you to feel stronger in that moment. And the more you continue to do this, the more relief comes to the rescue.

Typically, a thought pops up into your mind and by the time that thought exists, you've already popped over to another thought and another. Before you know it, you've already unconsciously chosen to agree and accept the thoughts that popped in as truth. This leads you to take action upon that thought, whether it be positive or negative. And here is the really good news: it's just a habit! Habits can be recreated at any point by making the choice and by knowing the benefit of that choice, and consistently choosing that choice again and again.

It's important to know that thoughts can swell really quickly. For example, maybe the thought pops into your mind that your best friend is mad at you. You don't actually know if this is true or not, but the thought popped up, and you chose to accept this negative-based assumption. The old mentality would cause you to perhaps feel sad because this friend is mad at you." *OMG what did I do? Why are they mad at me?"* You're now future-pacing and wondering about the next time that you see them and what you need to do differently. This can affect our nervous system, which will then cause panic, anxiety, nervousness, or worry.

Over time, if that thought habit continues, you then train your body to react immediately to that unconscious thought program. You see that friend or meet a new person and automatically your body feels panic. And you stand there wondering why you feel anxious during certain situations but not during other experiences.

I want to hold your hand through this and help you step far away from this hurricane thought spiral and automatic body conditioning, so let's do this together, okay? What do we do first? Become aware of the thoughts. Perfect. Next? Observe them. In a sense, hold the thought at arm's length and give it a good look over. Ask yourself if you want to attach yourself to this thought and accept it or entertain it as true.

If not, you can tell yourself: *"No thank you. That's an old thought. That's not 100% true. That's not me. That's not something I want to believe in. I have the power to choose a new thought."* By telling yourself these things, you are being the caretaker for a part of you who is scared. You can stand in that strength without judgment and give love and comfort to a part of you who deeply craves it.

Please hear me when I say that this WILL become a learned behavior. And when we're learning a new behavior, we want to make sure that there is a reward system to it. As humans, we make two different choices, and those are to either increase pleasure, or to decrease pain. Every habit that you have does one of those two things.

If you have a habit of negative thinking, that is not who you are. This is just a habit that you have. When the thought rolls in, please do not judge that thought or feel shame. When we cast judgment on ourselves, it only decreases our self-esteem and motivation. You didn't have the information at the time to heal and redirect those thoughts, but now you do!

"OMG, why would I ever think that? I'm such an idiot."

Again, this is where we can step in as the caretaker. A negative thought pops up in our minds, and we say: *"Okay. That's a thought. I don't like that thought and I don't want to associate myself with it. That's an old thought. I am safe to think something different, I hold all of the power."*

Then immediately change what you are doing to distract yourself from that thought. Call a friend, watch a show, go for a walk, and my favorite? I put my wrists under ice-cold water. It immediately switches my state of being and calms my nervous system. This is an example of immediately redirecting and switching a behavior. Now, let's think about how this changed behavior is now benefiting you. Going back to the reward system— you're now leaving that negative thought behind, which is decreasing pain, and you are also increasing the pleasure in your life with whatever it is that you're choosing to distract yourself with. I talk about this all the time with my students. They'll say things like:

"I just feel so stuck."

"I'm so overwhelmed."

"I just don't know what to do."

"There are so many opportunities I could choose, how could I choose one?"

When you say things like:

"I'll try..."

"Someday..."

"I could do this..."

"Maybe..."

Of course, we are never going to feel grounded or feel like we can move forward when we haven't made a definitive choice. I am going to share with you the 5 powerful words that will allow you to feel empowered and ready for inspired action.

I HAVE DECIDED TO_____BECAUSE _____.

This is a definitive outcome with a definitive reward system put into place.

"I HAVE DECIDED TO stop attaching myself to negative thoughts BECAUSE it will give me the chance to believe in myself more and that will feel amazing!"

Every time you reward yourself, you are encouraging that habit to keep on continuing.

See how much power you have taken back for yourself!? You allow yourself to become wildly aware of a thought, detach yourself from it, and you give yourself the power to accept or deny that thought as truth, and choose something different. These habits WILL change your life. If you start this NOW, you will create new habits, new behaviors, new ideas, new strategies that will allow you to increase your love for yourself. It will increase your motivation and allow you to feel better about YOU.

Some practical steps that you can take to begin this are these:

1. Create a kickass morning routine.

2. Create your "get to do list" for the day.

3. Prioritize your time.

4. Remain wildly aware of your thoughts and actions.

If we want more good in our lives, we need to make space for it! This means taking an energy audit on all things. We can no longer think, *"I am this way because of this."* We are now embodying powerful goddess energy and what does a powerful goddess do? She takes full accountability for her life. She is the mother effin' author. She writes the story, she chooses her energy wisely and she invests her precious energy in the right people.

YOUR CREW

And speaking of people.. I'm sure you've heard before that you're the sum of the 5 people that you hang out with most. If you want to rise in your business and create a balanced life, it is SO important that you surround yourself with people who will clap for you instead of judging you or dragging you down. You need people in your life who will encourage massive growth and who will be happy for you when that progress is made. If you want to embody goddess energy, who is holding you back? Who do we need to limit time with?

I want you to grab a pen and paper, or open up the note section of your phone. I want you to think about these questions.

Who are the 5 people that you are closest to? These are the people that you spend the most time with, the people whose energy influences you and your decision-making. I want you to write down their names.

Next, I want you to think about the time that you spend with each of these people, and I want you to become aware of how you feel when you are spending time with these people, and how these people leave you feeling when brunch and mimosas are over and you are headed back home. Do you feel stressed? Tired? Anxious? Not good enough? Like you are lacking something? Or maybe they are good vibes that you're experiencing. Maybe you leave feeling refreshed, excited, encouraged, pumped up. Whatever the feelings are, write them down next to their name.

Once you've done both of those things, I want you to look at each of the feelings that you wrote down and ask yourself if those are the types of things that you need in your life to help you progress on your journey toward healing and wholeness. If not, do you need to limit the time you are spending with certain people?

And lastly, I want you to examine the kind of friend that you are to your friends. Are you someone that brings light and joy to the conversation? Do you think your friends leave your house and feel refreshed and encouraged? It is so important for you to ensure that you have the right support system around you, but you can't expect everyone else to be a ray of sunshine to light up your life if you're bringing a grumpy Eeyore to the table. Be the friend to others that you want for yourself!

Really consider the results of this little exercise. The people that you allow to influence your life are going to do just that— influence your life! And you have 100% of the power and authority to choose what friends you give that privilege. I'm not saying that you necessarily have to start cutting people out of your life, though that may be the case sometimes. I am encouraging you to limit the time that you spend with those that drag you down. You can still love people while setting healthy boundaries and protecting your inner circle.

YOUR WORTHINESS

Maybe you have a new idea for your business. You want to scale up, try something different, or even just set more healthy boundaries within your business. Self-doubt can begin to creep in, and look something like:

"Who are you to do that?"

"No, you can't do that, you will probably fail."

"There's no room for you here, there's no way you can grow your business that big. "

There's doubt about your ability, which is really what self-doubt comes down to. When we break it down, there are two big factors to consider. The first are the thoughts that we are thinking. Why are you having these thoughts about growing your business?

Your thoughts are a compilation of past experiences, memories and come from the deepest part of your brain that is focused on keeping you safe. Your subconscious mind wants to make sure that it is run on the program that it has been taught to work on, and then, in turn, keep you alive. That is all that it cares about.

Maybe you think that if you were to show up with your business online, you wouldn't shine. You won't gain the following or interaction that you think that you should, and so you try to stay away. The interesting thing about your brain is that it is going to try to prove true anything that you believe within your core belief system. Your mind will delete and distort anything that goes against your belief, and it will narrow in on and focus on anything that supports the belief. Your brain will literally try to keep you within your projected reality all day long, even if there is an opportunity for you to grow and shine. It's really important to know that your brain believes that an opportunity or resource is false and so it will delete or distort any information contrary to that belief to keep you within your present reality.

The second big factor to consider when healing from self doubt is your confidence, which can be broken down into four building blocks as stated in the book, The Confidence Code by Katty Kay and Claire Shipman.

Self-esteem is that belief that you are a valuable person. You are valuable and worthy of really great things and experiences in your life. You believe that you are valuable to others, whether that be in your business or your personal life.

Self efficacy, which is believing that you have the tool to succeed.

Optimism, or I see an opportunity! Not pessimism which might believe that there is a problem in the opportunity, optimism is going to see the good that could come from it.

Self-compassion, when you are kind to yourself. The thoughts that pop up, you recognize that they are not you. Your subconscious really does want to protect you, and keep you safe. So, when you think about it from this perspective, you can think about the negative, bullying voice of your subconscious and actually soften that voice with self-compassion.

When I started thought work, I had horrible self-esteem and I found it helpful to think of that inner narrative as the voice of my daughter, Charlotte. I envisioned her scared and needing her mama. This caused me to approach that narrative with love and empathy instead of being cruel to it. When we attach a human to the voice, we can approach our responses differently. For example, if your child were to come to you scared, worried, or anxious about the situation that they were in, would you punish them and get angry with them? No, you're going to reassure them that everything is okay, mama is here with you to support you. This is the same way that you can respond to the voice of your subconscious mind when those self-sabotaging thoughts pop in. Reassure your brain with compassion and love.

You have to be very mindful of the way that you are talking to yourself. It can be so natural to let it just happen, but it is absolutely vital to implement self-compassion and to be consciously aware of the way that you speak to yourself. The way that you talk to yourself is actually rooted in two things; your existing inner narrative and your self-esteem. These are going to determine whether you have self-compassion or if you talk down to yourself and allow toxic, negative thoughts to enter the scene.

If you see yourself as worthy and capable, then you are going to talk to yourself as such. The things that you believe about yourself and the things that you believe you are capable or worthy of are going to have a significant impact on your self-esteem. This is what I call your identity: how you see yourself. And when your identity is challenged, when you're faced with a situation that is in conflict with what you believe to be true about yourself, your self-doubt will begin to rise.

I was first a hairstylist and after many years in the industry, I opened my own salon. Through the process of shifting from a hairstylist to a salon owner, I would feel constant guilt and anguish. I did not see myself as a salon owner or a leader. I still believed that I was just a hairstylist, so I couldn't see myself in any other light. I couldn't see myself leading other people because I didn't believe that about myself. It wasn't a part of my identity yet. Self-doubt was creeping in because my identity, or beliefs about myself were being challenged.

This is something that I teach my clients, and something that I want for you as well: you have to rebuild your identity of who you are. By giving yourself full permission to rebuild your neural network around how you see yourself will give you so much more ease. If you can learn to see yourself as someone who is thriving, making more money, and as the future self that you are working toward, then you can begin to relieve some of that guilt and self-doubt that you are experiencing. You can alleviate procrastination, self-sabotage and begin to navigate through the changes that growth brings.

YOUR CONFIDENCE

Some people may believe that if you have high self-esteem, then you must also have high confidence. But sometimes, that's just not the case, because confidence can be broken down into many aspects. You may think that you're not a confident person, that's just not your personality, etc. But the truth is that there are some areas of your life in which you ARE confident, and other areas that you're just not quite sure of yet. I don't like to generalize confidence as an overarching thing that you are not currently embodying. I call bullshit because I know that there are areas of your life that you are confident in! Maybe you're confident in your cooking skills, but not in your decorating skills. You're confident in your people skills, but not your math skills. You're confident in the way you write, but not when you have to speak in public.

I KNOW that there are things that you are confident in and I believe that identifying the things that you aren't confident in will give you so much more clarity on those areas where work needs to be done. Can you even build confidence? That's a hell yes. Let's talk about how.

Maybe you're naturally a risk taker, or maybe you're naturally more shy and reserved. Neither tendency is going to make it impossible to build confidence, but it helps to know your natural DNA so that you can learn how to approach confidence building for your unique situation and identity. Once you can identify your natural tendencies, you can then begin to specify and pick out which areas of your business you feel confident in, and which you don't.

If I sat down to talk with you, I know that there would be some areas that you are pretty kick ass in. If you were to give yourself credit, you would realize that you're probably really good at a lot of things! You just may not be very good at identifying those things or giving yourself proper credit for them. It can be difficult for women to give themselves credit where it is due, because we don't want to come across as too strong or bold. So much of this can be traced back to how we were raised, the people that spoke into our lives, the way that they treated and talked to themselves, and us. If you, for example, were raised by someone that had an issue with negative self-talk, there is a big chance that you picked up on that and continued that in your own life as well. And that habitual, negative self-talking behavior is going to have a major impact on your confidence.

One of the biggest issues that is causing resistance when we are learning to build our confidence is self-compassion, or self-love. If you have a tendency to punish yourself when you fuck up, it is because you want to be good and successful and accomplished. We punish ourselves because we think that this is the way to increase motivation toward success, but the truth is that when we punish ourselves, we are actually decreasing motivation, inhibiting growth and lowering self-esteem. I know at this point you may feel like self-love is still too difficult to obtain and that's 100% okay. What I would like to suggest is that you can see it yourself neutrally so it's not good or bad, it just is. Eventually, if you stay neutral long enough, you will start to ease on the side of like, and then into love.

This means that it is time to reverse engineer our minds. We may tend to keep pushing to achieve in hopes that it will make us feel more confident, optimistic or have more self-compassion but the truth is that no amount of success alone will make us feel confident. We already have to be full of optimism, self-confidence, self-efficacy, regardless of the things that we accomplish. We have to understand that if we mess something up, it's no big deal! Learn from it! Try again later.

When we have filled our inner cup of self-compassion and love for ourselves, the things that we accomplish are just going to cause that cup of confidence to overflow even more. When we try to fill our confidence cup with success, what happens is that even when we do accomplish our goals and can finally see ourselves as successful, we will still feel empty because we never learned to love and fully accept ourselves. We are so often trying to build confidence from the wrong place and when we do this, we will still question ourselves, still lack clarity, and feel unsure. And when this happens, we won't be able to take action, we don't believe in ourselves, and we end up saying "no" to ourselves, our family and the people that we love, because we are too afraid and lack the confidence to take control and create boundaries.

Here is my question for you: What would your business look like if you had self-confidence or even self-neutrality? What would that change, what would love or being neutral change? And how would this directly affect you? Would those changes be worth it? I hope that your answer was an astounding "*HELL YES!*"

YOUR RELATIONSHIP WITH ABUNDANCE
AND MONEY

The truth about manifestation is that you're already doing it right now. Manifestation is the end result of what you have been thinking about, feeling, your habits, and what you're taking inspired action with.

"I want to grow my business."

I hear this all the time.

"I want more clients, I want more product sales, but it's just not happening. Maybe I should try a new product? A new marketing strategy?"

You start questioning your business, you start questioning yourself, you stop showing up online because you're nervous or you don't feel adequate, and then you end up feeling even more lost and resentful. I want you to understand the power of your inner universe. The truth behind getting more clients and product sales is that it starts with the things that you are thinking. There is actually a science to this all, there is science behind how your thoughts can shape your reality.

I am willing to bet that around 85% of those reading this are running on someone else's program. What I mean by that is that your beliefs around success, money, business, your goals, your income limits, actually come from someone else's beliefs. They're not originally your own. Like we have talked about before, people that raised you, society, etc. have created a limiting belief system inside of you that is now holding you back in your business. If you're not making enough sales or gaining enough clients, I can guarantee that you are feeling stressed out, frustrated, worried, and nervous. You may wonder how your bills are going to get paid, which then leads to you wondering if this whole business idea was a mistake after all. *"If I just had predictable income, I would feel so much safer."*

I don't want you to feel this way, and I'm sure you don't want to feel this way either. The good news is, you don't have to. When you sit in sadness and worry, you are rooting yourself in lack and this low vibrational emotion will only cause you to think more scary thoughts. We've already learned about the hurricane thought spirals and that like attracts like, so when you are rooted in this low vibrational frequency of lack, you will only attract the same back to you. So, in essence, the worry, doubt, and sadness that you are experiencing is making your situation worse instead of better. You are attracting even more low vibrational experiences to yourself and I know that is not the end result you are looking for!

I want to challenge you with this question: What if it all went right? What if you had clients pouring in, you had $10k - $40k months coming in? Imagine this for yourself. What was your reaction? If it was something like, *"oh that could never happen for me. That would take too much work."* Then we need to start challenging and becoming aware of your beliefs around abundance.

If all of this abundance poured in, your thought processes around abundance, success, yourself, your worth, your abilities would be tested. Being able to grow your business is rooted in your relationship with these three components: money, success/abundance and being seen. Ask yourself these questions, and I want you to be really honest.

Are you okay with being seen as someone who is highly successful?

Are you okay with being someone who is making a huge impact in their business?

Are you okay with being seen as someone who drives around in an amazing vehicle, having the house of your dreams and going on adventure-filled vacations?

Are you okay with experiencing life in a whole new way?

Are you okay with being successful? Really okay with it?

I'm gonna spill the tea. You ready?

Business success is simply the byproduct of helping people and finding joy. And the more people you are able to impact and help, the more abundance you are going to be bringing into your life. That is all success really is. So, what if it all goes right? What if you found more joy, and helped a lot of people? Maybe success doesn't sound so scary anymore, but rather exciting and delicious!

I remember once, when I had first started my first business, someone said to me, *"You could become a millionaire!"*

And I scoffed.

"Ew, that's not me. I don't want to be that kind of person. I don't want people to see me like that."

I didn't realize it then because this was before all of my mindset work and intentional manifesting began, but my views and beliefs around money were flawed. Though I didn't realize it at the time, my beliefs around wealth were going to have to change before I would be in a position to receive wealth and abundance. This was the first time that I was challenged by my own belief system. The first time that I was cognizant of a belief system, or something inside of me that was causing physical resistance in my body. All of the excuses, the procrastination, I was holding myself back from truly impacting people in the way that I deeply longed to.

I eventually learned that my beliefs of money were adopted from my parents' beliefs around money. We always had enough for family vacations and to live comfortably, but we were never extremely wealthy. I remember conversations about those who were rich and they would say things that implied that wealthy people are simply not *who we are.*" I believed on an unconscious level that if I made more than what my parents made, I would be seen as someone who could not be accepted by my family. I grew up and had those unconscious beliefs associated with wealth, and I definitely didn't want to be seen differently. On a primal level, I desired love and acceptance just as any other human does.

When you are able to change your inner universe, change the things that you believe about abundance, you are able to change what you receive. This means that you can have massive abundance and wealth once your inner universe is rewired! Once your inner light is shining and is no longer shadowed by your preconceived beliefs and your limitations, you will begin to be freed from that inner resistance that you are experiencing inside your business.

First, change your inner universe. When you learn to believe that more good IS COMING, you believe that you are worthy of it, worthy of receiving, worthy of light, love...When you can see that for yourself, and believe that it is coming to you, it will. At lightning fast speed.

So, how do you start? I don't want you to just start rattling off affirmations. I want you to reassure yourself that more clients and product sales are on their way, even though it doesn't feel like it right now. More clients are coming, more products are selling, my bank account is filling up and I am so beyond grateful. The nervousness and worry that you might be feeling? That's just temporary. Good is on the way— so much of it.

Use your most powerful tool, which is your imagination, and imagine that this is all happening. The funny thing about your brain is that it doesn't know what reality is and what is just you using your imagination to create a scenario. So, when you close your eyes and begin to imagine the good flowing in, you will begin to vibrate at a higher frequency, which is what is going to attract those things that you already believe are on their way.

MARKETING YOURSELF

Maybe you're feeling a little nervous about how to show up in your business and how to talk about the products and services that you provide. Most likely, you started your business to help people. Whatever your business looks like, your market is people, and what you are offering to those people is going to change their lives for the better. I can bet that you are really good at what you do, and you have already begun to help people inside of your business. And this—helping people...that's what I want you to focus on in this section.

If you're already in business, then you've already begun to help people! What you may need help with is learning how to talk about your offer and how you help people. I want you to think about the people that you have already helped with your business. Maybe you've been in business for 3-5 years now, and you're already helping people. I want you to think about the top 3 people that you've truly helped that have walked away from your business with really amazing results. I want you to embody this for a moment and how you've helped these people, how you've made their lives easier or how you've helped them shed light, or feel beautiful.

Maybe these people had tears in their eyes, maybe you have lifelong friendships with these people. Whatever the case was, I want you to think about those results. That— those results, that's what your client cares about. They want to know that you care and that you are going to help them get the best results that your business can offer. And if you've done it three times, or hell, even once, then you can do it again and again.

One of the big hang ups that people have with marketing themselves or talking about what they have to offer, is because they don't know who their audience is. They don't know who their target market is. They're shooting into the wind and hoping to land clients. It gets really challenging to be clear about who it is that we are serving when we try to serve EVERYONE. If you're serving everyone, then you aren't really serving anyone. When your target market is too broad, it becomes impossible to craft a product that will help all of them.

We have to find who it is that we are talking to. We have to find those we connect with so that those who we are serving will feel seen and heard.

"Ah! She's talking to me! She hears me! This is what I need."

Instead of going around and telling everyone what it is that you have, you can connect with people by making them feel heard and loved. Offer them a solution that you have that will enrich their lives. This is what people want. They want someone that will understand them, love them, hear them and solve their pain points. And when you can figure out who your people are, what they are struggling with, what their needs are, what's keeping them up at night, and when you truly care about them, that's when you will be able to serve them and offer them something worth having.

This is how you build your tribe. It's not just about the money, it's not just about selling more and making more profits, it's about helping people. It's that simple. Just help that person in the most authentic way that you can, and avoid focusing on how you can make more money. The byproduct of helping is MONEY. The more you help people, the more trust that you will build with people and the bigger your community will grow.

So first, we are thinking of the people that we have already helped, embodying those results and becoming rooted in those successes, and then leading forward with those results. Next, get clear about who it is that you are trying to reach and help. Super, super clear. And then speak to the issues that they are struggling with and talk about what it is that you have that can truly help them.

No one likes a sleazy salesman. In fact, if I just say "sales," you probably get a creepy-crawly feeling and you think about a car salesman that wants to rip people off, or those people in the mall that are trying to interrupt your stroll to rope you into their latest and greatest product. We have all sorts of negative emotions attached to selling, and I believe that this is why we often have a hard time with selling our business.

This is why it is so important to know who your market is, and to fully understand what it is that they are struggling with. I cannot emphasize this enough. If you don't understand the person you are trying to help, and you don't know what it is that they really need, then you aren't going to be able to confidently offer your services to them. You won't be able to confidently make claims about your product and how it will affect their lives for the better, because you don't know if it actually will or not. And then you end up feeling like a phony salesman at the end of the day.

Do your market research. Research, research, research. What is it that these people are struggling with? If you can craft a product that is a kick-ass solution to your tribe's issues, then you are going to feel more empowered and confident to wake up every day and offer your services to these people.

So how do you confidently talk about your offerings? You first have to nail down these 2 things: Who is it that you serve? How is it that you are helping them?

The reason that I started my company is because I wanted to show that I am a shining example of what is possible for you. I didn't start my business or write this book without first having done all the work myself. I've experienced it. I am a small business mama. I have battled depression, suicidal thoughts, anxiety, and an eating disorder. I have struggled with lack of clarity, I have felt the need to show up inauthentically, as someone who I'm not and it only made me feel more lost and, in turn, more anxious and depressed.

I know the struggle because I've been right there with you. Until I changed it all. I had little to no self-worth or self-compassion. I've swapped all of those thoughts and now, I believe that I am worthy of everything. I am not afraid of receiving abundance, or afraid of how people will view me.

I long to help you along the same journey that I have been on, because I know what it feels like to be where I was, and I know how amazing it feels to be where I am right now. And that's what I want for you, too. Yes, it will take work, but it will be refreshing, encouraging, and a big weight will be lifted off of your shoulders when you revitalize these energies and learn to become the more magnetic version of yourself.

And not only will you begin to feel better, more authentic and more self-confident, but you will begin to see massive growth in your business that couldn't come about any other way.

Chapter Eight/
The Letting Go

"Faith that it's not always in your hands or things don't always go that way you planned, but you have to have faith that there is a plan for you, and you must follow your heart and believe in yourself no matter what." -Martina McBride

It was like a bad dream that she couldn't wake up from. The pain was deafening. She was out of touch, out of control, and the world was spinning around her. Everyone else seemed like they had it all together. Why couldn't she be like everyone else? It seemed like everything that she had put her heart into was gone. This isn't the way things were supposed to go. She worked so hard. She planned. She had imagined the life that she wanted and she knew what it would take to get there.

She had imagined it all: a modest home in the city with 2 kids, a white picket fence, and maybe even a mom minivan eventually. You know the dream, and she imagined doing it all with him. He said he would never leave, never cheat, never love anyone else. And now all of those words and promises rang hollow in her ears as she contemplated what her future could possibly hold now. Now, she couldn't see past the pain and the sadness.

What now?

If only she could have taken a peek 7 years into the future. Where all of those dreams and more were her new reality. Maybe the pain would've stung just a little bit less had she known just how much the Universe, God, the Divine, had in store for her. It was more than she could have hoped for. It was sweeter, it was...just right for her. She didn't know it at the time, but that heartbreak was the incident that propelled her toward her destiny.

Now, she can look back on those lonely, painful days with a smile and a glimmer in her eyes. That memory of pain, and the beautiful life that she now experienced would come back to her mind again and again when she faced adversity. Because she knows that that part of her story, though it seemed like the end, was just the beginning.

Maybe you have a dream, a wish, an idea of what your life should look like, and you're working your ass off to get there. You're encountering resistance, yet you're doing everything right. You keep thinking, *"why is nothing working?"*

You make detailed plans to hit your goals, you put in the time to meditate and throw out the negative thoughts. You have everything under control. You've energy audited everyone and everything. And now...What else is there? Is there something you're missing? You've crossed your T's and dotted your I's. Why isn't the abundance flowing in yet??

I say this in the most loving way possible, but if this is you, maybe you're trying to be too in control. You're energetically not trusting in the Universe, God, or Divine to send abundance your way. You're working all on your own strength and trying to will your perfect life into existence without acknowledging where these good things are coming from.

What if your ideal life, the life you think you want, isn't actually the best path for you? What if the universe has something even better in store for you, but you're so invested in controlling your own destiny that you aren't leaving any room for the Universe, God, the Divine, whatever it may be that you believe in, to send you the abundance that you truly deserve.

When I teach the law of attraction, I realize that it may be especially appealing to those who identify as control freaks.

"You mean all I have to do is clean up my thought life, work on my belief systems and I can receive everything I want?!"

Well, yes, but also, no. Not exactly. It can be easy for some of us to slip into manipulation instead of manifestation. We want to micromanage every part of our lives, and we try to do everything we can to make things go our way. But then, sometimes, it doesn't just happen like that. Our perfectionism is tested, and then ensues the anxiety and frustration because your perfect plans aren't playing out like they're supposed to.

I'd like you to now adopt this new thought; you are the co-author with the Universe, God, and the Divine. This isn't a one-woman-show. This is you, aligning yourself with a powerful energy and putting yourself in a position of readiness to receive. And, of course, taking inspired action. That's how you do it! And as long as you are intentionally aligning with the goal you want and it is in fact for the greater good of you and others, it will make its way to you.

My number one piece of advice is this: release the expectations of what you think the outcome should be and what you think the process should look like. Receiving what you want doesn't always look pretty and perfect. Sometimes it looks messy as it makes space for this new thing to exist in your life! Trust the process, it's all working for you.

Manifestation doesn't require overthinking and although our mind is a magical gift, it's not actually where you find your highest power answers. Use your brain, yes. But when you are trying to align with your true self or trying to learn about how the universe works and how to get good things to come your way, it can get confusing and even frustrating. And that's where you are going to head back to a place of meditation and stillness so that you can hear that voice of truth within you that will guide your steps and show you the way.

If you're the logical type that loves to know the ins and outs of how everything works, you're going to wear yourself out trying to understand the magic of how the universe works. At some point, trust comes into the equation and we learn to accept that some things just work because they work. This is where your feelings are allowed to flourish and they work to keep you in the loop and point out when you are experiencing resistance. It's not all black and white, it's full of all hues and shades of color.

I mentioned earlier that the energy of control comes from a lower energy vibration, and this is because the need for control is rooted in fear and desperation. We're scared to fully let go, we're unsure or nervous about letting fate decide, and we're afraid of any other idea of "good" except for the idea that we create. We can get tightly wound up by trying to control every scenario and outcome and we have convinced ourselves that we know what's best. We know that the universe has good in store for us, but is it really what we want or what is best for us? Maybe we are just not quite trusting that the universe has the very best in store for us and something even better than we could have ever imagined is on its way!

When this is happening in our lives, when we are letting perfectionism and the need for control take over, we are setting up roadblocks between us and the abundance that is coming our way. When fear is in charge of our actions and emotions, that is a low vibration energy. And what happens when we are emitting a low vibration energy? That's right, we attract even more of that vibe back into our lives. That's not what we want! That's exactly what we are working so hard to AVOID! So what the heck do we do now?

When we encounter these fears, we have to work to bring those fears to light and expose the root of the issue so that we can learn how to correct those belief systems and learn to trust and surrender to the experience. Why are we afraid to let the universe have a say in our destiny? Maybe you're the kind of person that likes to do everything on your own. You've pulled yourself up by your bootstraps and made it this far on your own! And that's great, but there is a much better, more freeing way to go about bringing abundance into your life.

Let me just say that learning to counter our controlling tendencies doesn't mean that we are giving up all power over our lives and giving control to the wind. No way. I've just taught you 7 chapters on how to gain control of your mind, emotions, and ultimately, your life. The best thing I ever learned is that the only thing I have control over is my behavior. The more we can lean into that thought process, the more we can release the external situations happening around us, and lean into our own mind.

There's always a balance to all of this. I don't want you to give up your dreams or stop putting in the intentional work, I just want you to learn to simply trust the process, trust the universe, and trust the good change that is coming. And most importantly, trust your damn self.

I want you to run with inspired action toward your goals, and along the way, I want you to trust that your work is going to pay off, because you are in alignment with the universe that is bringing abundance your way as you are pursuing it. Obsessing over your desires isn't the answer. Worrying about whether or not it will happen isn't going to speed up the process. The worry needs to go, the obsession needs to go, and the only solution is to,

"LET IT GOOOO..."

We've been over this before, friend. Worry just causes resistance, and it is a sign that you don't really believe that abundance is on its way. If you truly believed that it was, then why the heck would you be worrying about it? Let go of the how, let go of the when and begin to live in a state of constant trust. Jim Carry said it best when he said,

"As far as I can tell, it's just about letting the universe know what you want and then working toward it while letting go of how it comes to pass."

Letting go and trusting allows us to be released from the negative thoughts and the energy of desperation. When you are trusting, you are no longer living in a low vibration energy. You are living in the energy of acceptance, faith, and gratitude. And that's the exact place that you want to be.

What obsessive/perfectionist thoughts and desires have you been experiencing? I want you to write them down and be vulnerable. We're getting really deep up in here, but that's where the healing is done. Are you afraid to let go? Do you trust your own mind more than the Universe, God or Divine? Do you believe that they have the best in store for you? Because they do, whether you believe it yet or not.

Trust. That's my message to you in this chapter. Trust. I'm not necessarily talking about just trusting in yourself. I want you to trust in something bigger: the universe, God, the Divine...whatever it is that you believe in and believe is supporting and guiding you...I want you to learn to surrender to that.

The reality is that everything we have manifested into our lives has come by way of the universe. Let's take a manifesting audit. Take a look around you. Are you in your car, house, business office? Everything that you have around you is a result of your thoughts, feelings, actions. Manifesting is exactly the materialization of what you believe you are capable of achieving.

There are signs all around you that are guiding you and pointing you in the right direction. I have been talking with a lot of my friends and colleagues who have had trouble getting out of their thoughts and stepping into trust. Being able to surrender to this experience and releasing the expectations of what should happen to make room for something even more beautiful to evolve. You may think that you want something and you may be hustling hard to achieve it. You may even feel deep in your heart how badly you desire this, but what if the universe, God, Divine actually had something even more magical in store for you?

If it's not working and it's roadblock after roadblock, then trust that there is something pacing you. There is something setting you on a new path or direction to ensure that you are exactly where you need to be. Forcing things is not only going to be difficult, but it won't be enjoyable either.

Let's say you're an online entrepreneur, you're a hairstylist, esthetician, photographer, whatever you may be. Let's say no one has booked in a week, or you haven't made any sales yet this week. The schedule is looking spotty, sales are down, and you begin to panic. Anxiety is creeping in and maybe your old money story begins to show back up. Old belief systems that you thought you dealt with are beginning to show their faces again.

First of all, I want to make it clear that worry does NOT change the end outcome. But what it does do is it gives you an opportunity to think about where the root of the worry is buried, to heal and to trust that good is on the way. You can take inspired action and not trauma-based reactionary action. I'm speaking entirely from experience here. I've had traumatic money loss, unfortunate money issues and years of deep worry around money. I had to learn to trust when things were slow and to avoid trauma-based reactions to get a temporary feeling of safety.

I want you to understand what I mean by trust, so consider this scenario:

Let's say there's a drought where you live. The rain has dried up, the flowers are heavy from dehydration. The flowers are beginning to wilt, the grass is brown instead of it's usual lush green. You're not thinking that the rain will never come again. You don't assume that you'll never see a blooming flower again. You know that it's just a season. It's just a phase, everything will be okay.

That innate trust— knowing deeply that everything will be okay...that's the kind of trust that I want you to have within your business. Just because this season may be slow and sales may be low doesn't mean that this is where you will be forever.

You already know this from experience. Think back to another time in your life when things seemed dismal, but ended up turning out for the better. Maybe there was a relationship that you thought would last forever that turned toxic. You were lost, but now you've found your true soulmate that you know was made for you. Maybe you lost out on a business opportunity that caused you to dig deeper, market more, and you landed an even bigger gig that couldn't have otherwise happened.

What is your story? Pinpoint a time that the universe has proven to have your very best interest in mind. And that, my friend, is the proof that you need to cling to when the days get tough. Reminisce on the times that things actually worked out for the better. You are already supported right this very second, and I know that there is proof of that in your past that can encourage you today.

What is your story? What messy situation has turned into a beautiful story in your life? Maybe it was something unexpected that you didn't have to work toward. Something that wasn't even on your radar that just fell into your lap. Maybe there was something that you never thought would be possible for you that actually happened.

Write it down. Cling to that. That is the proof that you can hold on to. You are not blindly trusting. The Universe, God, The Divine, is never changing. What it has done for you in the past, it will continue to do for you throughout your life.

I want you to remember that when you do take action, I want you to take inspired action that is rooted in trust. The second you get a sale or a client booked, you will suddenly feel like everything is great again. But that is a temporary feeling of safety. What we really need to focus on is that when things do slow down, you don't slip into feelings of reactionary trauma. I want you to fully trust that this is temporary, you will continue to take inspired action, and that you are always safe, in any season.

When those clients do start trickling in, you want to think:

"Ah, there it is. I knew it was coming, I was waiting for you."

And not,

"Oh thank God, I was beginning to panic."

The energy of trust is like knowing that the rain will come again. Maybe the grass is brown, maybe the trees are bare. But that's okay because it's winter right now. Spring will come again and everything will be lush and green. This is the energy of abundance.

When you come from this space, things are going to feel so much better.

So how do we learn to trust? Ask yourself, *"What am I afraid is going to happen if I don't make as much money?"* You will get the response and then ask yourself if this is 100% true. At this point, a part of you may actually believe it is. But there is a part of you that calls bullshit on that answer and that's the person you want to lean into. You will tap into awareness and say, *"The abundance I am looking for is also looking for me. I am releasing any blocks between us."*

At this point, find time to be still. Sink into your higher self and crawl into the warm arms of the universe. There you will find the safety of surrendering.

Chapter Nine/
Manifesting it All

"When you visualize, then you materialize. If you've been there in the mind, you'll go there in the body." -Dr. Dennis Waitley

Friends, we've made it a long way and you should be hella proud! We have removed all of the weeds, we have tilled the soil, we've prepared the ground and it's now time to begin to plant our seeds of abundance and watch them grow and flourish. I'm going to break this down for you step by step.

As we go through this process, you may be excited and tempted to try all the things at once. But I want to remind you to stay patient and lean into the trust that we have built. We have made it too far to step back into the low vibrational energy of desperation. At this point, in order for your manifestation to arrive, you must believe in yourself and in the inevitability of good that is coming your way. The key to manifestation is to set it aside and forget it. Have the belief, focus on your daily growth and take inspired action.

Do one or two of the following methods daily, not all of them! We're not here to microwave our way to abundance, we're using what I call, The Crockpot Method. Do you ever constantly worry if the food you put inside the crockpot is going to be cooked when you get home by the end of the day? Probably not. You set the timer and you trust and KNOW that by the end of the day, you will have a beautifully cooked meal. That's the energy that we want: the energy of trust and ease. Take action, and then go on with your day with a deep understanding of what's coming. Strong and steady is how we are going to make this ish happen.

SETTING INTENTION & ASSIGNING GRATITUDE

Before we dive into manifesting, we first have to set very clear intentions about what it is that we want to manifest. Wishy-washy hopes and dreams aren't going to cut it. We need clear, straightforward goals that are intentional. What is it that you want to attract and call in? More money? Your dream car? More clients that understand your value and pay your worth?

Think about and decide what that thing is. Do you have it down? Do you know what your thing is? Once you know the intention, I want you to ensure that it is SUPER clear. You want more money? Well, what are we talking? Fresh Benjamins in your hand? A larger figure on your bank balance? More investments or money to send your kids to college? I want you to see it clearly in your mind. THIS is the thing that you want to attract.

Once you can see it, I want you to change your dialogue and set this in the present tense. *"I can't believe I am making $1,000 a day!! My clients are giving me $200 in tips a day!! My bank balance is $100k!"*

See the difference? We're not saying *"I want to make more money...someday I will make more. Someday I'll be able to afford my dream car."*

No, ma'am. Do we want abundance *"someday?"* No! When the heck is someday?? That's not clear or intentional. We want abundance NOW. We're changing our perspective and trusting in the universe. And we have so much trust that we can refer to our goals in the present because we fully believe that they are already on their way!

Have you ever been in a cave, or a big empty room? You can yell out something and the echo will bounce back to you, reflecting what it is that you put into the space. That's how I want you to picture this manifesting process. The universe is going to echo back what it is that you put into this space. If you're shouting out words like *"someday"* and not setting your goals in the present tense, that's what is going to be echoed back to you.

"Someday I will make a lot of money!"

And echoed back, *"Someday I will make a lot of money!"*

These aren't the results that we want and this is why I want you to set your intentions in the present tense. And once you do this, I don't want you to miss this extremely important step. We are going to assign intense gratitude and joy surrounding it. Gratitude is the biggest secret to manifestation. Gratitude and joy are some of the highest energy vibrations and when you assign these, you will see a massive improvement not only in your manifestations, but in your life as a whole.

Do you like people that just take, take, take? No, of course not! And the universe doesn't either. ASSIGN GRATITUDE. Thank the universe in advance for the things that are coming to you!

"I am so happy and grateful that I am making $1,000 a day!!"

MENTAL REHEARSAL: USE YOUR
IMAGINATION

This is the fun part. This step is called Mental Rehearsal.

Did you know that we are the only creatures on the planet that have the ability to imagine? What a gift! To get lost in a book, a story, even just our own imaginations, and enter into a whole new world, new time, new reality. When this happens, our brain picks up on two things: what we see and what we feel. Have you ever used a virtual reality headset and gone on a roller coaster? Yeah. That ish feels real!

This same concept works with manifesting. If you close your eyes and imagine your intentions happening, then you assign emotion to it, your brain won't know that this isn't already your reality!

Try this right now: I want you to close your eyes and imagine that your intentions are a reality right now. Your dialogue is going to change a little bit more now. I want you to say out loud, *"I AM SO HAPPY AND GRATEFUL THAT I AM MAKING $1,000 A DAY!"* Make sure to jump, clap your hands, celebrate and be in the moment of it actually happening!

You see what we have now? We have our clear intention, we have set it in the present tense, and we have assigned both gratitude and positive emotions to it.

What will happen in your life when your intentions are a reality? I want you to imagine all the things that will be possible. The stress melting away and off of your shoulders. Roll your shoulders back now, doesn't it feel great? You will pay off your debt, you will book your dream vacations, you will have more than enough to provide for your children and to give them the life that they deserve. Doesn't it feel good? I want you to do this exercise every single morning until the doubt finally leaves you.

Remember when we talked before about Hebb's Law? I'm going to remind you, because it's so important and this is the science behind what this exercise is doing for you. This is neuroscience.

Hebb's Law is that, *"nerves that fire together, wire together."*

Every time you have a thought or emotion, like *"I am so grateful that I am making so much money. I am so happy that I am helping so many people!"* Your emotions, which in this case are gratitude and happiness, are tied to the thoughts of abundance. What you're actually doing is creating new neural pathways around the reality of abundance and wealth.

By attaching positive emotions to these thoughts, you are intentionally wiring your brain to create your neural circuitry, which is the way your brain will habitually operate and produce your reality.

In other words, you're rewiring your own brain to create new habits, which will then turn into actions and then produce your new reality. You can wire your brain to live a reality that doesn't exist yet and this is the exact energy you emit that signals the law of attraction.

DO THIS EVERY MORNING!

LET'S GET VISUAL

This might be the most fun part of this manifestation process: a vision board. If you've never made one of these, girl, you are missing out! A vision board is a visual representation of the things that you are manifesting, and it is a powerful tool to help you in the process of visualization.

Your vision board is your picture of the future. Your hopes and dreams, your goals and wishes, all put into picture form and made into a collage that is put in a place that you will often see. Your vision board is a snapshot of your ideal life.

The idea is that since our brains are highly visual and respond well to visual stimuli, when you create a vision board that is made up of images that evoke a strong emotional reaction, you will be strengthening your high vibrational energy, which will, in turn, begin to activate the Law of Attraction. Once you have defined your intentions, it's time to get visual.

First, I want you to decide on a place where your vision board will exist. This should be somewhere in your home or office where you spend a lot of time. You want to be reminded of your intentions as often as you can, so that they can remain at the forefront of your mind. Maybe that space for you is your office wall, your kitchen, on a nightstand beside your bed, wherever it is that you choose, just make sure that you are spending a lot of time in that space.

Once you choose a space, choose your medium. You can use a cork board, a white board, a piece of plywood, etc. There are even places where you can buy professionally made vision boards, but I like to make them myself because I end up putting a lot more time and effort into my boards, which is, of course, more thought and energy that I am putting into my manifesting.

Collect pictures of what you want to happen in the next 3-6 months. They can be images that represent certain emotions, experiences, and physical items that you want to attract into that time frame. You can use stickers, magazine cut-outs, images printed from Pinterest, photographs, anything you want. Then you can also add affirmations, words or quotes that inspire you and make you feel gratitude and joy.

We don't want to attract chaos into our lives, so be intentional about your board. Put only the things that you clearly know that you want to attract. Make it beautiful, simple, clear, and make your intentions easily seen on your board. You want to be reminded of your intentions at a glance.

If there are many different areas of your life that you are working on manifesting in, I want you to create multiple vision boards. Don't try to cram it all into one. You can create one for your financial goals, one for your relational goals, and one for your business. There's no limits to what you can and can't create vision boards for. Like I keep emphasizing, just be intentional about them.

Once your board is complete, I want you to make a habit out of meditating on your vision board for a few minutes every day. Since it will be in a place that you will often see, you will also be reminded frequently of your intentions. And when you are, I want you to pause, breathe, and imagine your intentions as your current reality.

You can even review your board before bed every night so that you can trigger your subconscious mind to focus on those things while you sleep. The time right before you fall asleep at night is especially powerful for manifestation because the images that you view in the forty-five minutes before you fall asleep are the things that your subconscious mind will replay over and over again throughout the night. This practice will cause you to wake up with a burst of motivational energy and new ideas surrounding your goals.

ASSIGN FAITH

At this point, you know your intention and what it is that you want to attract into your life. And now that you have this idea clearly seen in your imagination, it's time to release those expectations of what your ego expects the outcome to look like and allow God, Divine, the Universe to create something even more magical for your future.

I know this step can be met with a little more resistance than the others, so I want to give you a step-by-step for this.

Place your hand over your heart and wait until you feel its predictable rhythmic beat.

Place your other hand directly below your first. This is your solar plexus chakra, where your creativity and personal power live.

Close your eyes and breathe deeply.

Imagine your intention like you do with your Mental Rehearsal, but with a new emotion of sureness. Your intention will happen. It's already on its way right now.

Then say, out loud, "*I know you are on your way, and I am ready with open arms for you.*"

This statement is heart centered and fueled with faith and trust. The moment you allow yourself to sink into the knowing of your being, you will unknowingly release control.

777: A MANIFESTATION TECHNIQUE

The 7X77, also known as 777 manifesting technique, is a practice of repetition designed to reprogram your subconscious mind to create thoughts that will match the energetic frequencies of your desires.

Here's what you do: write out one desire that you wish to manifest with gratitude and in the present tense. But don't just write it once, write it 77 times each day for 7 days in a row. This technique is a form of hypnotic writing. It allows you to see the outcome of your intentions on repeat and the subconscious mind begins to create new measurable networks anytime you attach the emotion of achievement with the visual outcome of your intention.

Remember, anything you experience on repeat, whether positive or negative, is taking a toll on your subconscious mind whether you are consciously aware of it or not. The 777 approach to manifesting allows you to harness the power of repetition, neural networking and Hebb's Law and to make it work for you to create the future that you desire.

THE FOCUS WHEEL METHOD

This is one of the most powerful methods that you can use when setting your intentions and manifesting. When you begin to construct your personal focus wheel, you may find that you discover new intentions that you want for yourself that you weren't aware of before. You may discover that you have greater clarity around your existing intentions, and that you gain an overall better understanding of your intentions.

A focus wheel is a large circle that reaches almost the edges of the paper you are drawing on. Inside the large circle, draw a smaller circle. Use the space between these two circles and divide it into 12 equal parts (like a pie), leaving the inner circle blank. This is your format.

Next, set your intention. What is it that you intend to manifest? Is it related to abundance? Maybe you desire financial abundance. Inside of those 12 segments, I want you to begin writing sentences about your life that begin with, "I love." What things about your current life do you love? Maybe you love your spouse, you love your kids, you love your home, your office space, whatever it is, construct a sentence around that thing and the abundance that it provides for your life, and place one sentence in each of the 12 segments.

"I love my partner and the abundant love that they show towards me and my family."

"I love my kids and the joy that they bring to my life is rich and abundant."

"I love my warm and inviting home that provides space and comfort for my family to grow and thrive."

I want you to think of 12 things that you can ascribe gratitude towards, but I want you to be intentional about this and choose things that you would like to see an increase of in your life. The goal is to be grateful for things that you currently have an abundance of in your life.

Once you have found your 12 things, you are going to place your greatest intention in the middle space. Maybe your greatest intention is financial abundance, so you are going to write something like, *"I love how supported and equipped I am to provide financial support to my family."*

Once you've created your wheel, it's time to use it. 3 times a day, I want you to stand in front of your focus wheel and to read aloud the "*I love*" sentences from your board. Start with the 12 outside sentences, and I want you to say them in an excited and animated way. No monotone, our brains know when we're faking it. If the sentences that you chose for your board are true, then there will be authentic excitement and joy that you will feel as you are reading them off.

Once you've read the outer 12, and you are grounded in gratitude, I want you to repeat this 3 times. Yes, read through each of these aloud 3 times in a row. Once you've done it three times, I want you to read aloud your greatest intention that you wrote in the inner circle.

Chapter Ten/
The Celebration

"When people believe in themselves, they have the first secret to success." -Norman Vincent Peale

That's it. We have made it to the final chapter. We have been through so much through these chapters, and I wish that I could know you personally and could hear how you have become the author of your new story. I know that it would be beautifully unique and I am privileged that you have made it this far into this book. I hope that the things that you learned here will stay with you throughout your life. I am honored to think that I have played even a small part in enriching your human experience. I know you have amazing stories to tell, and even more amazing things that are coming your way. Things that you have intentionally manifested, things that you deserve, things that you have worked so hard for. And contemplating it all just makes me smile.

I wish I could sit down with you, hear what your biggest takeaways were, your struggles and, of course, your victories! I know how beautiful your journey will be because I have experienced it for myself. And I can't wait for you to experience the same in your life.

If only we could sit down together over a warm cup of coffee and share my thoughts and hear yours too. But since that's not realistic at the moment, we are going to practice one of our visualization techniques. I want you to grab your favorite beverage. I'll be here with mine. Grab a blanket and cuddle up on your couch while I share with you my final thoughts.

Everything I shared with you in this book was intentional. I was careful not to share anything unimportant. I value your time and I don't want to throw fluff at you and hope for the best. As you read through this book, every single detail, technique, and piece of advice was written for you.

And all of those things are great, but if there was only one thing that you took with you from this book, I would want you to leave with a full understanding of how important it is to choose yourself, to honor yourself and to prioritize yourself. None of the rest of this stuff is going to matter if you miss this one thing. You have to choose yourself.

When you choose yourself, all of the other things that you are working toward will fall into place. There are a multitude of reasons that choosing yourself is important, but I want you to focus on these 4 key reasons with me.

First, when you choose yourself, when you honor yourself, **you will dream bigger**. You won't be caught up in what others will think. You won't worry about how your goals and dreams will affect others. When your priority is yourself, your dreams will be more daring, more intentional and much more exciting. The limitations will be removed and you will be free to follow what it is that you truly want. You will dream and create from a larger perspective, because you know how empowering it feels to believe in your worthiness. When you believe that you deserve more, you'll go for it. Bigger dreams equals more abundance, more creation, and more expansive experiences.

When you begin to choose yourself, it is very common for you to feel as if you are being selfish in putting yourself first. What about your kids? What about your partner or spouse?

I want you to consider those in your life that mean the most to you. Is it your other half, your children, maybe your parents even? Consider those people. Would they benefit from your abundance? Heck yes they would! Your kids will benefit when you are bringing in big bucks, your partner or spouse will benefit when you receive financial freedom and are able to manage your own schedule. Your parents will benefit from a daughter who is financially (and mentally and emotionally and spiritually) stable. Everyone in your life that you care about will be directly impacted– in a good way, by your choice to put yourself and your wellbeing first.

When you choose yourself, you are going to work more intentionally, receive a bigger abundance, and in turn, have the freedom to give generously to those in your life that you care for. It's a win-win situation for all of you. But it has to start with you having the courage to say, "You know what? I choose myself today."

Not only will choosing yourself make you dream bigger, but **it will give you increased bravery that is needed to chase after those big dreams**. When you understand your worth, you will be willing to fight harder for what is already yours. When you consistently honor yourself, you start to believe in yourself. You'll know that you are capable, that you are worthy, and will be confident enough to pursue the opportunities that come your way.

So many times we are held back by our own view of ourselves. We don't believe we deserve abundance, so we don't pursue it. We don't believe that we deserve financial freedom, thousands in savings, or the house of our dreams. And it's all rooted back in our view of ourselves. Maybe all that is holding you back from abundance is the bravery that comes when you learn to choose yourself.

When you believe that you are worthy, you will have the ability to receive self-acceptance which will increase your magnetism. Self-doubt will decrease your energetic vibrations, while self-acceptance and love will increase those vibrations. If you remember back to former chapters, higher vibrations are what we want. You will soon be attracting the energy that you are emitting and magical things will begin to unfold for you. When you truly choose yourself and believe in your worthiness, you will scientifically increase your vibrations, which will, in turn, increase your abundance.

If you haven't been convinced yet that you need to CHOOSE YOU, allow me to keep going. I have a few more thoughts that I want to leave you with.

When you choose yourself, when you honor yourself, **you are actually opening your energy to receive the things that God, universe, or the Divine is sending directly to you**. There are unlimited resources in the universe. This reminds me of the small business loans that became available during the COVID-19 Pandemic to provide relief for small businesses. If you needed that money, you had to hop on it quickly because there were limited resources. Only those that got their application in first were able to benefit from that limited abundance.

That may be the way that the government works, but not the Universe or God! There are unlimited amounts of abundance that are accessible to you at all times and to access it, it begins with knowing you are being divinely protected. It's about releasing the worry,the fear or the what if's and taking inspired action toward the life you deserve. By choosing to honor yourself, better yourself and invest in your future, you are telling the universe that you are open and ready to receive the good things that it has for you. The universe is vast, abundant and beautifully generous. It is up to you to be ready to surrender and receive it.

I want you to live in such a way that will leave you with no regrets. At the end of your life, I want you to look back and say, *"That was a good fucking ride."* I want you to know that you were brave, took chances, and created a life through your creation. I don't want you to stand there with regret or thoughts of what would've happened had you taken this whole manifestation thing seriously and chosen to invest in yourself when you had the chance.

No what-ifs.

I want you to have truly lived, full of intention, full of love, full of gratitude and joy, self-acceptance, and a deep understanding of your worth. That's what I want for every one of you reading this book.

While loving yourself is the number one thing that you need in your life to bring abundance, fear is the number one thing that will hold you back from receiving your intentions. Fear is the number one thing that will lead you into a life full of regret and it's the only thing that holds anyone back from taking inspired action. Fear of failure will cause you to never even try. Fear of success will keep you from giving it your best. Fear of what others think will cause you to dim your light and tiptoe around the person that you were born to be.

Once the brain feels fear, it will build a story to convince you to cower down and make you afraid of taking action even more. Don't let fear lead you into a life you will regret. You have the power and the tools now to properly release that energy and embrace gratitude, joy, and love for yourself.

You don't have to be afraid of your own inadequacy when you know your abilities and you know that you are constantly working on bettering yourself.

You don't have to be afraid of the future or of uncertainty when you have learned to trust that the universe, God, the Divine, has your best interest in mind.

You don't have to be afraid of rejection when you know that the right doors for you will open exactly when they are meant to.

You don't have to be afraid of being judged or afraid of how others perceive you when YOU love who you are.

You don't have to be afraid of missing out when you know that you are exactly where you are meant to be.

You don't have to be afraid of getting hurt when you know that emotions and feelings are a part of what makes you human. Forming meaningful relationships and investing deeply in a cause will disappoint you some days, but that means that you are alive and fighting.

I want you to take inspired action and put the what-ifs behind you. Don't just do something to do it, but take steps that come from your soul. The key to taking inspired action is by building your bravery muscle. Little by little, your fears will melt away and be replaced with a strong, brave woman who knows exactly what she's capable of.

I get it, this stuff can be scary. I was exactly where you are right now. I didn't transform my life in a day. There were many things I was afraid of, things that I had to work through, and things that I had to release and rework within my subconscious. Everyday I am still doing the work to release the conditioned parts of me. It's a lifelong journey that will be the best and most inspiring journey you will take. And I'm not asking you to do this all in a day. Or even all in a year. All I'm asking you to do is to take one step forward, and then keep on the path.

Even teeny tiny steps in the right direction is PROGRESS and that's what we want. This is the act of taking simple action steps toward the goal of exercising and building your bravery muscle. Even if it's something as simple as joining a FB group, googling, doing research, any step towards the goal is going to start building the bravery muscle. Little by little, that's the way we do it.

I want you to leave with this: be empowered. Believe in yourself. Surround yourself with people who encourage you, who cheer when you succeed and who have your back when you don't. Nourish your mind, body and soul. You are a wholly complex creature, embrace that and learn to honor your full self. I want you to live this one life with intention and purpose.

Go and be who you were born to be.

Printed in Great Britain
by Amazon